BITSTREAMS

MATERIAL TEXTS

Matthew G. Kirschenbaum

BITSTREAMS

The Future of Digital Literary Heritage

PENN

UNIVERSITY OF PENNSYLVANIA PRESS

Philadelphia

Published by
University of Pennsylvania Press
Philadelphia, Pennsylvania 19104-4112
www.upenn.edu/pennpress

Printed in the United States of America on acid-free paper
10 9 8 7 6 5 4 3 2 1

Library of Congress Cataloging-in-Publication Data
Names: Kirschenbaum, Matthew G., author.
Title: Bitstreams : the future of digital literary heritage / Matthew G. Kirschenbaum.
Other titles: Material texts.
Description: 1st edition. | Philadelphia : University of Pennsylvania Press, [2021] | Series: Material texts | Includes bibliographical references and index.
Identifiers: LCCN 2021007047 | ISBN 978-0-8122-5341-2 (hardcover)
Subjects: LCSH: Bibliography —History —21st century. | Literature and technology. | Digital media —Social aspects. | Bibliography —Methodology. | Literature —Research —Methodology.
Classification: LCC Z1001.3 .K57 2021 | DDC 302.23/1 —dc23
LC record available at https://lccn.loc.gov/2021007047

To my colleagues and students

at the University of Maryland

Contents |

Preface | Actual Facts

What are the prospects for bibliographical knowledge when literary texts (and the material remains of authorship, publishing, and reading) are reduced to bitstreams in the global data flow? What are the opportunities—and obligations—for book history, textual criticism, and bibliography when literary texts are distributed across digital platforms, devices, formats, and networks? And what do the critics, historians, biographers, bibliographers, editors, designers, publishers, librarians, archivists, curators, dealers, collectors, prize committees, educators, and the general readers who together steward literary heritage need to understand about the role of computers in the composition, production, distribution, and circulation of today's texts? Indeed: what is textual scholarship when the "text" of our everyday speech is a transitive verb as often as it is a noun? These were the questions that gave rise to the chapters in this book in their initial incarnation as the 2016 A. S. W. Rosenbach Lectures in Bibliography at the University of Pennsylvania.

The bitstream of my title is a term of art in computing, where it denotes any contiguous sequence of bits for storage or transmission. A file is thus a bitstream. In the parlance of digital preservation, the term takes on an even more specific meaning: a bitstream is a complete copy and surrogate for all data contained on some unique piece of storage media, sometimes also known as an "image" (as in a disk image or a hard drive image). In 1998 the historian R. J. Morris had predicted that "within the next ten years, a small and elite band of e-paleographers will emerge who will recover data signal by signal."[1] He was to be proven right. (And the analogy to paleography is perhaps even more apt than Morris realized, for the electromagnetic waves that fluctuate between physical storage media and the symbolically rendered ones and zeros of digital computation are as individuated as any majuscule.) We will explore this specialized usage in what follows, but I also mean the bitstream to encompass the vast sea of digital data we encounter every day. The bitstream in this more capacious sense is defined by the extent of our bandwidth, the strength of our signal, and the nodes of our networks.

By literary heritage, meanwhile, I have in mind collective prospects for archives, public memory, and scholarship in the face of what Virginia Woolf, writing in *Three Guineas* (1938) in a prior era of technological change, called certain "actual facts."[2] For Woolf, the actual facts were the availability of the tabletop platen press, the spirit duplicator (or ditto machine), and the typewriter—innovations that helped change the shape of literary production in her lifetime, as she knew firsthand. For us, the actual facts are the ubiquity of desktop and laptop computers as instruments of literary composition and revision as well as book layout and book design; new forms of publication and distribution, including ebooks, audio books, print-on-demand, web, and transmedia works; the profusion of literary conversation online (authors accessible on social media, critical commentary on blogs, and the massive store of readers' reviews and rankings on sites like Amazon or Goodreads); and finally—not least—the particulars of the contemporary literary archive, combining as it does physical artifacts with digital assets or objects, the bitstreams of the latter stored on individually owned media and devices but also (increasingly) in the remote recesses of the cloud.

Of course, there are innumerable *other* actual facts that *also* have bearing on contemporary literary production. Woolf (in fact) made her remarks to an epistolary interlocutor in the context of the pernicious influence of editors, editorial boards, and publishers on the distribution of printed matter to the public. In our own moment, such influence is manifest in everything from legislative policy and court rulings over net neutrality and internet privacy to the copyright and contractual arrangements that govern our online transactions with human and algorithmic agents alike; and they are arguably far more systemic and totalizing than anything with which Woolf had to contend. (Witness Amazon's infamous deletion of *1984* from its Kindle devices over a decade ago in 2009, or Google's abrupt removal of *The Weaklings*, a long-running literary blog by the writer Dennis Cooper.)[3] Literature has never been its own separate sphere, and such parochialisms are even less tenable when the bitstream is piped to our devices and screens by the same information architecture that delivers search results, voice calls, or cable TV.[4]

Track Changes (my previous book) was also very much about bitstreams and literary heritage, but there those concerns were subordinate to the historical narrative of word processing I sought to relate. Here, by contrast, I have tried to consolidate my thinking about digital technologies and their relationship to bibliography, textual criticism, and book history. In part, I regard this present work as a kind of sequel to my first book *Mechanisms*, taking up (in the guise of the bitstream) once again the intertwined effects of what I termed formal and forensic materiality, but refracted through the narrative style I adopted in *Track Changes*. But the more immediate predecessor in my writing is an essay entitled "Operating Systems of the Mind," given as an address to the Bibliographical Society of America and published in *PBSA*.[5] I concluded it by asserting, "bibliography itself is not bound to particular media, methods, and tools: it is instead a habit of mind, one we consciously adopt so as to avoid conjuring the mind's own printers—and now too, operating systems of the mind." *Bitstreams* picks up where this address left off, with a direct appeal to the particulars of media, methods, and tools, as well as to habits of mind. My approach here is informed not only by textual studies and bibliography, but also the contributions of media archaeology, software studies, and platform studies—critical frameworks that have collectively reshaped the conversation in media studies since that field underwent its own material turn more than a decade ago. (As I have written elsewhere, book history increasingly shades into media history.)[6]

While the three lectures as given at Penn shared common themes and common purpose, it will be helpful to know that each was intended to be its own occasion. Accordingly, each rested on a distinct conceptual formation, discursively fixed by a definite article. These were: the archive, the computer, and the book. And yet, the first premise of the lectures was really that each of those definite articles was a fiction. Archives, computers, and books are multitudinous in their material variety.

Since that time, my thinking has evolved still further, particularly as this book goes to press in the midst of a pandemic that has refocused our attention from the transmission of innocuous bits to the transmission of a deadly and life-altering virus. It also goes to press at a moment of intense social and political action acknowledging truths about America's racialized and racist present and past. But the questions with which I began have not gone away, as the impact of the foregoing on literary activities online attest. We have seen, for example, a surge in ebook readership as public libraries and bookstores shuttered.[7] Likewise, the activities of Black writers, Black publishers, and independent Black booksellers have all come into new focus through (especially) Twitter and other forms of social media, with sales reflected in the *New York Times* bestseller lists.[8] The consequences of the pandemic and the fight for racial justice—actual facts in their own right—should embolden us to speculate about how and why bibliography (as well as the ultimate question of literary heritage) will continue to matter.

All three lectures have been revised significantly since their public deliveries, which are still available to view on YouTube.[9] The first, on the archive, has been rewritten entirely—the work on Toni Morrison is all new, and little of the actual lecture remains, though some of it is now part of the Introduction. The contours of the basic story I tell about William Dickey and Kamau Brathwaite are intact in Chapter 2, but my study of both has progressed significantly—most notably for Dickey by seeing his digital poetry through to its long-deferred publication at the same time I was finishing this manuscript;[10] and for Brathwaite, a much fuller understanding of the environment around early desktop publishing and digital type, including participation in a summit on the desktop publishing industry convened by the Computer History Museum in May 2017.[11] Indeed, my work on each poet has swelled their respective sections to almost the length of a lecture apiece in their own right, which explains why Chapter 2 is now the longest. Meanwhile Chapter 3 (on Abrams and Dorst's *S.*, or *Ship of Theseus*) has benefited immensely from the large project I took on immediately after the Rosenbach Lectures, a research investigation and a white paper entitled *Books.Files: Preservation of Digital Assets in the Contemporary Publishing Industry* (2020).[12] The Coda, which acknowledges the extraordinary circumstances of the year 2020, is also entirely new. I hope readers find that the incorporation of my ongoing work in so many different registers contributes to balancing this book's distance from its originating occasion.

Introduction | The Bitstream

L et's begin with a new file: File → New. Let us say the person at the keyboard is a poet, in the early stage of what is eventually to become a five-part work, referentially dense but comprised of lines and phrasings that are sharp, resonant, and memorable—so much so that in future years, much later in this century, the poem is widely seen as capturing the zeitgeist of this tumultuous moment, a text of indisputable literary and historical significance embraced by diverse constituencies as among the most important and influential of its age. Let us assume that this text becomes the subject of seemingly inexhaustible critical interest, the centerpiece of dissertations and monographs, of commentaries and interpretations. English majors (yes, there are still a few) can quote from it, and certain of its lines and phrases enter into popular circulation on refrigerator magnets and greeting cards and such.

Of course textual interest in this work would be intense, with those scholars who are attentive to such things concerned to establish the relationship between the poem's various sections, extant drafts and versions of each, their sequencing, the identities of persons who may have first read and helped revise them, and so on. Exactly the sort of questions, you may have recognized, that for many years animated inquiries into T. S. Eliot's *The Waste Land*.

Those questions have now been answered, though the definitive work on the topic, by Lawrence Rainey, was not completed until nearly a hundred years after *The Waste Land*'s initial printing and some three and a half decades after facsimiles of the poem's manuscripts and typescripts were first made available by the poet's widow, Valerie Eliot.[1] In the interim, several scholars had tried, and failed, to establish a sequencing for the poem based on its textual evidence. Why had Rainey succeeded in their stead? He knew that Eliot tended to buy his writing paper in small batches and that he used it indiscriminately, for literary drafts as well as for correspondence and household needs alike; the archival availability of Eliot's letters (with their dates) allowed him to compare their paper stock to the surviving manuscripts and typescripts, thereby establishing the various "strata" (as Rainey terms it) of the poem's composition in ten distinct layers. Along the way, he also solved the mystery of the different typewriters that textual critics had long understood Eliot to have used during the poem's composition but whose conflicting typographical evidence had confounded their attempts to order and date the typescripts by measuring ascenders and descenders with coffee spoons. Astonishingly then, it was not until quite recently that literary scholarship could offer an authoritative answer to a question as basic as in what order were the various sections of what is arguably the most famous English-language poem of the twentieth century composed.

Why bother seeking answers to such questions, one might ask. Rainey responds by quoting Ezra Pound: "The more we know of Eliot, the better."[2] This is the same sensibility that Jerome McGann calls the scholar's art, or as I have elsewhere put it: we don't always know why we want to know some things, but we know we would rather know them than not know them.[3] It is the impulse that led early modern savants to compile enormous folios of reference works (430,000 words here, 10 million there), as Ann M. Blair has meticulously chronicled.[4] These are, in other words, the sorts of questions certain constituencies of scholars have always sought the answers for, and they have done so out of the conviction that knowledge is not instrumental and that we can never know when or why or in what context seemingly recondite facts and expertise will be deemed suddenly urgent and essential. But what would it take for someone sometime in the future whose motivations were like Rainey's to bring the scholar's art to bear on the twenty-first-century masterpiece I have conjured with my opening hypothetical? Rainey, after all, had access to actual papers in archives that he could evaluate as physical evidence; what will remain for an intrepid coterie of e-paleographers who find themselves working on my notional text two or three generations from now?

Let us say that the first file the poet opens when she begins writing is a new Microsoft Word document. Almost instantly, shadow copies of the file begin to proliferate on the magnetic hard disk servicing the old Windows laptop she still favors, in temporary caches and virtual memory throughout the operating system. Because the laptop is also synched to her Dropbox account, the file is duplicated on a server array in a remote data center whose location will likely never be known. This is the basic working document for the text, and as the poet writes she freely deletes and revises on the screen in front of her, with no particular thought for keeping records of the text's version history (the Track Changes option is off by default). But she doesn't just compose ex nihilo—she finds the blank screen and blinking cursor too foreboding—so she gets the process started by copying and pasting text from unfinished drafts and fragments, some created years beforehand on even earlier computers. On a number of occasions throughout the writing process (which will last for many months) the text is dumped to the laser printer at the poet's office at a nearby university. Though printing through the internet is of course possible, the poet has never bothered setting up the VPN connection it requires; besides, she likes the ritual of saving the file to a portable USB drive or even emailing it to herself to download onto her office computer—running a newer version of Windows, a more recent version of Word (which is accessed through her institution's cloud service), and outfitted with a solid state as opposed to a magnetic hard drive.

On more than one occasion, the poet begins editing and revising this derivative copy only to catch herself, whereupon she must then carefully key a duplicate set of revisions back into what she now thinks of as the original or master copy of the poem. Versions of the file with suffixes like "to-print-Tuesday" proliferate. They proliferate on the laptop, on the USB stick, on her office machine (and its remote file system), in Dropbox, and in her email account. Over time, these versions all capture the text in states that are eventually effaced by the ongoing revisions to the master file. The printouts, meanwhile, are also marked up by hand, and inevitably some composition takes place in the margins or on the back side of the pages. (The poet attaches no particular mystique to working longhand but will do so when the opportunity presents itself.) These emendations too are keyed into the master text, though they often change still further in the process. The hard copies are placed into a file drawer for the most part, but not always—more than one ends up on the floor of her car.

Eventually the poet is ready to begin sharing her work with a long-time confidante and writing partner. She emails the file to her friend—call her Esmeralda—who chooses to open it in her Google Drive account. There Esmeralda begins editing, using the service's commenting feature at times but also liberally rewriting the text itself since Google Docs saves all version information by default and can roll the user back to any prior textual state. After Esmeralda has finished, she invites the poet to access the shared document as a collaborator. They spend several intensive sessions working through the changes, each accessing and editing the document from their own computers, sometimes accompanied by a telephone (or Skype or Zoom) connection, other times availing themselves of Google's built-in chat feature. Indeed, several particularly troublesome lines are finalized only through live back-and-forth real-time editing in the chat window, each watching the other's phantom cursor moving as if at its own behest.

This collaboration is intense and intimate and at times fraught, but the poet is accustomed to it—she used to hand hard copies back and forth to Esmeralda when they both lived in the same city, where they would meet in coffee shops to workshop one another's writing. (As she says, Esmeralda is better at the craft.) In any case, the text is shorter now by nearly half, but she believes that it is to the good; the poem now has shape, direction. She's able to see it with the dispassionate eye that she knows is the sign she's almost ready to let it go. At this point the poet's partner also reads it on an iPad he takes with him on a business trip to Lausanne; he finishes it at a café overlooking Lake Léman and offers some additional edits; this time the file is saved, modified, and backed up in an Apple iCloud account.

Not long afterward the completed text is sent onward to an agent and then an editor (conveyed as a simple email attachment—the poet, who remembers wrapping and shipping her first manuscripts at great expense through the post, still marvels at how quotidian that final operation is in the wake of so much effort), from which point it is further edited, copyedited, and proofed, versions and copies proliferating across yet more computers, email accounts, and online services. When it is at last ready for typesetting, it will be imported into Adobe InDesign, which will explode the Word file into a cluster of interconnected layers and assets, including fonts and style sheets. The InDesign files will then be transmitted as print-ready PDFs to a print production facility somewhere in the American Midwest, where high-speed web-fed offset presses will perform an initial run and actual printed sheets will be cut, collated, and bound, from there to be put on trucks to distribution centers. A separate firm with which the publisher contracts will create files to various types and specifications for the still non-standardized ebook market. The publisher, incidentally, maintains all its digital assets on storage leased from Amazon, as does the printer.

Enough! (Or too much.) Though the scenario I have been sketching is fictional, I trust it is recognizable as the basic textual condition we all encounter on a more or less daily basis, assuming we write with the benefit of a computer and an internet connection. The scenario, in other words, is not exceptional or extraordinary even if it is reminiscent of a certain predecessor text in some of its particulars. Here are some key points I would wish to bring in to focus. First is the extreme proliferation of the text in all its various versions and states. As Cory Doctorow puts it, computers are machines for copying bits.[5] Strictly speaking, a file is "copied" each and every time it is opened or accessed since the operating system is reconstituting it from low-level data structures, which get stored on the media. Each revision of the file is thus also a multiplication. But beyond that, the effortless ease with which we copy files—sometimes just to move them from one device or network to another—means that textual scholars confronting a work such as I have described will have no way of knowing how many copies of a certain text may actually be extant, or where they are located—often, as I have suggested above, they will be on systems to which the scholar and archivist cannot hope to obtain access, whether technically, legalistically, or logistically speaking. And they will likely number in the hundreds, at least.

Second, notice the cross-pollination of different services, platforms, and file formats: Microsoft Word, multiple versions thereof; Google Drive; Apple iCloud; Windows and Macintosh operating systems, with multiple varieties of each; storage and transmission via fiber optics, wifi, magnetic, and solid-state media; and finally, of course, hard copy. Each of these services, platforms, and formats has its own internal architecture, its own technical protocols and functional idiosyncrasies. It is true that files usually transfer seamlessly across platforms and networks, and most of us, going about our daily routines, undertake such transactions without a second thought (and if something does go wrong, it is immediately noticed and quickly remedied). Nonetheless, it is also worth acknowledging how much tolerance we have built up for the routine glitches and incompatibilities that are in fact indicators of exactly the material processes of transmission that textual scholars will need to become attuned to in the future: the glyphs and symbols we sometimes encounter in an email message or a file attachment, for example, are artifacts of the gaps that still persist between different character-encoding standards. For most of us these are minor annoyances or curiosities; to the bibliographer, however, they offer clues and insight into the systems and software used to compose and transmit the text.[6]

Next there is the question of the files themselves as digital entities: how do we determine their structure and extent as objects of bibliographical inquiry? In the case of a Google Docs file, for instance, is the object at hand some particular state of the text, or is it the document in its temporal entirety—each revision, no matter how trivial, available to anyone who has access to the account that created it in the first place? What about comments and annotations, or embedded chat transcripts? What about the style sheets associated with a Microsoft Word document? What about the kind of metadata that is always attached to digital files but typically invisible to the end user? What about remnants of past versions and states accessible only via forensic analysis of a hard drive? We know that electronic documents are date- and time-stamped, and increasingly they are geo-located as well. (How much easier would Lawrence Rainey's work have been if all Eliot's files had been tagged to the second in Greenwich Mean Time!) But these values are also volatile, as files move across the many varieties of systems just described, continually opened and closed, copied and renamed. Copying a file on Windows operating systems will update its creation date, for example; copying a file on Mac OS X will not.

Finally, of course, there is the question of exactly what the author herself might have chosen and been able to save in the first place. We have learned that our poet—whose life is, after all, as busy and chaotic as anyone else's—is not above leaving annotated drafts under the seat of her car. Will she really continue to meticulously migrate her files from one computer to the next, keeping old drafts up to date as standards and formats change? Will she ever sit side by side with an archivist and allow that archivist to systematically harvest the contents of her Google Drive and social media accounts? How many of us can even remember the names of—let alone the passwords for—all the online services we have ever signed up for, if they are even still in existence? And then there is this: many of us—including prominent writers employed by universities—do not even own our own computers; they are loaned or leased to us, and our old machines (which may or may not be scrubbed of personal data) are absorbed into the global e-waste industry at regular intervals. This is where computers, which are ultimately as disposable as anything else in the planned obsolescence of the consumer economy, revert back to the rare Earth minerals from which they came, even as their non-reusable and non-degradable components accumulate in open-air landfills. Licensing agreements and the lifecycles of institutional IT assets may have more of an impact on the future of literary heritage than any of us yet appreciate.

Given everything we have just rehearsed, it might be tempting to forego any hope of recovering any bibliographical evidence at all. We would presumably be left with the text of the poet's work as it was published and perhaps those hard copy printouts in the file drawer I mentioned (but not the ones that wound up under the seat of the car). Maybe that's okay? It's more or less what survives from *The Waste Land*'s composition, after all. Why should we hold out hope of being able to reconstruct some delicate trellis of electronic data any more than we would harbor the expectation of harvesting an author's eraser shavings in order to reconstruct an expunged word originally written in pencil?

A more constructive answer might begin with differentiating the media and modalities of computer storage across several different historical eras. Recovering data from a ¾-inch magnetic DECtape reel (as would have been used on a PDP-10 mainframe) is a very different proposition from retrieving it from a 3½-inch diskette or a SATA hard drive, and each of those cases present different circumstances from data stored with a contemporary cloud service. These are not peripheral or incidental details to what being digital means: for all the portability and transferability of digital information (what the industry terms "device independence"), there is no computation without representation—by which I really mean inscription. Indeed, the need to reckon with the material particulars of storage media is a minor but persistent thread in foundational documents of computer science. John von Neumann, in the opening pages of his *Draft Report on the EDVAC* (1945), acknowl-

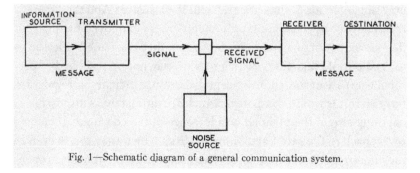

Fig. 1—Schematic diagram of a general communication system.

1 | Claude Shannon's 1948 diagram of a general communication system. Note the unlabeled box (the "channel" or "mere medium") at the very center. *The Bell System Technical Journal* 27 (July 1948). Reused with permission of Nokia Corporation and AT&T Archives.

edges the necessity of consigning data to some physical substrate or material; he refers to this as the system's "organ."[7] Soon thereafter, a diagram in Claude E. Shannon's "A Mathematical Theory of Communication" schematically depicted the flow of messages from sender to receiver. Shannon's corresponding model of information, in which "meaning" is independent of the mathematical integrity of the message, underlies essentially all modern communications and networking technology, from the telegraph to the packet switching of the internet. Here though I wish to draw attention to the central box in Shannon's diagram, the one unlabeled in its original presentation. That blank box stands in for what is "merely the medium," as Shannon describes it in the text, or the "channel" through which information—what we are here calling the bitstream—must flow. "It may be a pair of wires, a coaxial cable, a band of radio frequencies, a beam of light, etc.," he adds.[8]

Since then, computer systems design has had to account for the physical properties of paper, magnetics, laser light, and electrical charges, as well as more exotic materials such as mercury delay lines and cathode ray tubes. A key proposition of this book is that those material necessities, which (from Shannon's perspective) are "merely" a medium to be out-engineered—ever faster, ever more reliable, ever more capacious, automated, and invisible modes of storage—also *and* simultaneously *and because of* the friction and resistance inhering in that very materiality—become our hedge against oblivion. In other words, the actual physical properties of different kinds of media, though collectively rendering the bitstream vulnerable to fire, flood, deterioration, decay, incompatibility, obsolescence, and other forms of calamity—are *also* what give us our only real chance to find footholds for our future bibliographical interventions. Adapting William Morris, we might say we can't have preservation—memory—without resistance in the materials. Whether a floppy disk, a hard drive, a sheet of fanfold paper, or a spool of magnetic tape, storage media make up the non-virtual sites and surfaces where the bitstream takes on weight and heft.

Some storage formats and technologies are more challenging than others. But those in widest use during the personal computer era and the early internet era—ranging from 5¼- and 3½-inch diskettes to magnetic hard drives and CDs—all have reliable and relatively low-cost solutions available for reading and recovering data. A scholar or bibliographer who acquaints herself with the relevant tools and methods can therefore expect to be able to work with many of the most common storage formats from the late 1970s up until the advent of the cloud. From a strictly literary standpoint, this timeframe includes much of postmodernism and its aftermath, the decolonization of the literary canon, and the rise of brand-name mega-selling authors, among much else. The digital remains of literary heritage—the bitstreams—that attend this roughly thirty-year period are going to be recoverable as often as not, whereas material stored on earlier forms of digital systems as well as on more contemporary cloud-based media will be more fraught. Another argument of this book, then, is that it is important to begin acknowledging the periodizing effect of different digital technologies on the future bibliographical record.

But what about the code itself, all those ones and zeros that data and software are supposedly made of? Even if files and programs can be rescued from their dusty diskettes, can they still be read and reanimated on today's systems? Binary numbers are the lingua franca of computing—which is to say, the bitstream—because they possess two fundamental qualities: they are binary, and they are numbers. By virtue of being binary—one or zero, on or off—they can be used to implement the functions of Boolean logic; by virtue of being numeric they can be added and subtracted from one another, the formal basis of computation. As a result of what is really nothing more than a convenient system for encoding math and logic, what have historically been separate content types defined by their distinct physical properties—the silver halide gelatin forming the emulsive surface of a film, the groove incised in the wax cylinder by the motion of a needle—now converge in a common representational schema, the radical new ontology of the digital. All media—words and images, sound and moving images—are more or less equally susceptible to being represented in this way. Note that I do not mean to suggest that media are now immaterial—quite the contrary. But it does mean (as I argued in my earlier book *Mechanisms*) that in order to fully apprehend the import of the digital we must acknowledge that its technologies have been designed and engineered—often through excruciatingly precise tolerances—to create and sustain what I like to call an illusion, or working model, of immateriality.

As a function of the convergence of so many different media types in the bitstream, individual and collective data stores are now exposed to archiving, indexing, and algorithmic analysis, whether the data in question is voice, GPS, still or moving image, or text. But this radical new ontology (as I have had the temerity to name it) also means that those data are fundamentally unstable, in the sense that they rest upon the foundations of *other* data—what is quite literally known as metadata—in order to be legible under the appropriate computational regimen (what I have previously termed formal materiality in my work). A given sequence of bits—a bitstream—thus has no essential meaning. A single byte (say 01000001) can be interpreted as the ASCII letter *A*, the decimal 65, or any number of other values, each determined by programmed logics that are themselves defined in the same exclusively relational way. Mark Hansen explains the implications of this situation:

> Arguably for the first time in history, the technical infrastructure of media is no longer homologous with its surface appearance. As distinct from phonography, where the grooves of a record graphically reproduce the frequency ranges of humanly perceivable sound, and from film, where the inscription of light on a sensitive surface reproduces what is visible to human eye, properly computational media involve no direct correlation between technical storage and human sense perception.[9]

In computer science, this effect is typically explained by way of recourse to metaphors like stacks and layers. As any textbook will tell you, the program layer rests on top of an assembly language layer, which rests on top of a machine language layer, and so forth—turtles all the way down, at least until we hit the hardware layer and the real-world laws of physics. It was for that reason that Friedrich Kittler famously declared there *was* no software, insisting instead that "all code operations . . . come down to absolutely local string manipulations, and that is, I am afraid, to signifiers of voltage differences."[10]

Kittler's fundamentalism is bracing. It is also technically accurate. But the irreducible reality of voltage differentials does not negate corresponding reality effects farther up the stack, and those layers likewise become points at which agency can be exercised and the bitstream arrested, sampled, and decoded. Emulation software, popular among computer gamers, helps demonstrate this: the actual physical circuits of outmoded consoles or computers are reimplemented as just another software layer, such that a bitstream image of some bygone game program manifests as a functional—*playable*—copy of the original instead of an undifferentiated chunk of binary content. The game neither knows nor cares about its absent hardware; indeed, for all intents and purposes, the hardware *is* there, it just happens to be there as software (that's the strange magic of an emulator).

The lesson here is this: the convergence of digital information in ones and zeros (or voltage differentials) notwithstanding, the bitstream is not homogeneous. Nor should it be unduly naturalized: decades ago, Sadie Plant argued that binary ones and zeros "offer themselves as perfect symbols of the orders of Western reality," embodying as they do "the ancient logical codes" behind our most elemental dualisms—light and dark, white and black, presence and absence, life and death, even male and female (she reads this last example in the very shape of the numerals).[11] Bibliography, I will argue—and the material sensibility of book history more generally, in keeping with the turn toward platform and infrastructure in recent media studies—gives us the habits of mind to begin seeing past the universal Western fiction of ones and zeros in order to bring the infinitely more variegated world of actual digital storage into view. For the purposes of this book, then, the bitstream is a phenomenon that exists *only* in so far as it intersects with its material supports and substrates. The digital *does* present a radical new ontology, but the particulars of that ontology are to be found in the bitstream's interactions *with* its material conveyances, not despite them. Emulation, for example, is never perfect, and its effects can be distorted by the speed of the chip in the host system, yielding a skewed and unfaithful—sometimes all but unrecognizable—representation of the original game program.

For the poet in our scenario, the outlook is mixed. Certainly whatever hard copy materials existed could be accessioned by an archives, and might provide clues and cues as to the digital devices and services that would also be of interest to posterity (consider the ways that directory paths are often included in the headings of a file printout). That USB stick on which the poet relied to shuttle files back and forth to her office machine—assuming it survived—could likewise be acquired by the archives, as could the data from the hard drives in her laptop and desktop computers (if anyone had the foresight to keep them from being reclaimed by the university that employs her). If such were to be the case, then a future e-paleographer might well be able to reconstruct portions of the composition and revision process in ways that could prove quite thrilling and far more granular than anything heretofore possible—literally keystroke by keystroke, all date- and time-stamped to the second. (One could even use an emulator to recreate her original desktop; exactly this has been done for one of Salman Rushdie's computers in the Manuscripts, Archives, and Rare Books Library at Emory University.) However the Google and iCloud and any other cloud-based instantiations of her work are more than likely gone for good, unless someone had taken very deliberate and proactive measures to safeguard them; we would be left with only circumstantial evidence of the crucial collaboration with Esmeralda. Relevant email correspondence may or may not remain, depending on how it was stored and archived; and digital pre-press materials, whether at the publisher or the printer, almost certainly will not survive.

That may sound like a discouraging assessment. But it needn't be. If there is no preservation without resistance in the materials, then we should also understand that where there is resistance, there will—always, inevitably—be loss. It's worth remembering too how precarious the circumstances surrounding *The Waste Land* manuscript really were.

It was believed lost until "discovered" by the New York Public Library in 1968 among the papers of patron and collector John Quinn. The manuscript of *The Waste Land* in fact consists of some nine different typescripts, carbons, and autograph copies, to say nothing of the miscellaneous letters and scraps of paper and juvenilia that Rainey relied upon to establish the timeline for the poem's composition. All these things endured not only because of the inherent material properties of paper and carbon and ink, but also because of a network of values that has been realized in institutions like libraries and archives, as well as a marketplace for rare books and manuscripts. (As Amy Hildreth Chen reminds us, the existence of literal markets for the papers of individual writers—shaped by Bourdieusian notions of taste-making and cultural value—may be the single most determinate factor in what gets "lost" and what gets preserved for scholarly uses.)[12] Any future literary heritage that encompasses digital materials must reckon with the inherent properties of magnetic storage media and computer software and operating systems; but it must also cultivate a commensurate set of values (including market value) to help ensure the persistent survival of hard drives and USB sticks as they are buffeted by the contingencies of time and circumstance.

For Donald F. McKenzie, comparing the new "textual forms" of computers to printed books in a 1993 address to the Bibliographical Society of London, the stakes could not have been clearer: "It is the *durability* of those textual forms that ultimately secures the continuing future of our past; it is the *evanescence* of the new ones that poses the most critical problem for bibliography and *any further history dependent on its scholarship*" (my emphasis).[13] Such a ringing declaration from a scholar of McKenzie's stature underscores the need for bibliography to come to grips with computer-mediated texts as the precondition for (and I quote again to emphasize) *"any further history dependent on its scholarship."* Yet we need not cede this ground to a swirl of evanescence or even the stark finality of Kittler's voltage differentials.

Bibliography, as McKenzie argued throughout his career, is not a discipline just about books, or even just about texts per se; it is a program of knowledge about what books and indeed all textual forms can "reveal about past human life and thought."[14] It accomplishes this through its uncompromising attention to conditions of meaning. Which is to say that bibliography is a way of knowing, a habit of mind whose remit is nothing less than accounting for all the people and things that make meaning possible, each in their own irreducible individuality. This is a book about computers and networks and files and formats, yes, but it is first and last a book about that habit of mind.

1 | Archives Without Dust

t's startling to see it on the Dell flat-screen set up lengthwise to duplicate the orientation of a sheet of paper: "BELOVED A NOVEL BY TONI MORRISON." These words are typewritten in the center of a badly burned page, barely legible through the discoloration of smoke and water damage. The edges are blackened and irregular; most of the top left quadrant is scorched away entirely.

I am looking at a high-resolution digital image of a hard copy printout of a working draft of the Pulitzer Prize–winning book. It is one of the manuscripts that survived the house fire that engulfed Toni Morrison's Grand View-on-Hudson residence at the foot of the Tappan Zee Bridge on Christmas Day in 1993. The crumbling pages have been conserved and scanned by the Department of Rare Books and Special Collections at Princeton University Library. Here *all* access to Morrison's papers—damaged or otherwise—is via digital surrogates viewed at a dedicated workstation in the reading room, network and USB ports disabled. (A note in the finding aid informs patrons that this mode of access is by request of the author.) *Pace* Carolyn Steedman, there is no dust in this archive and thus no risk of archive fever, at least not in any pathological sense.[1]

The haunting digital image in front of me registers as a testament not only to the resilience of paper and ink in the face of fire, smoke, and water but also to the efficacy of the collective array of memory institutions that ensure that treasures such as this are—in the novel's own parlance—passed on. Despite the screen that separates a researcher from the painstakingly preserved originals, it is easy to picture scholars doing much the same work they have always done: scrutinizing drafts for variants, poring over the author's correspondence, squinting to decipher handwriting on the pages of yellow legal pads. And the truth that such passings-on don't just happen by happenstance is one of the most

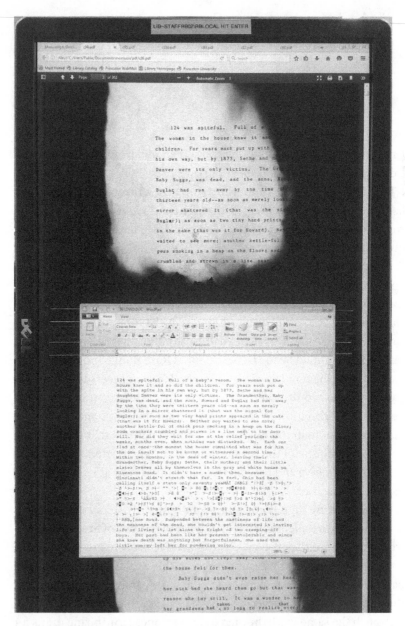

2 | Fire-blackened typescript pages of Toni Morrison's *Beloved* with a glitched portion of one of the Microsoft Word files created during the novel's revision process displayed together on screen in the reading room at Princeton's Firestone Library. Photograph by the author. By permission of the Princeton University Library, Special Collections.

basic lessons *Beloved* has to teach us. (Appended to a different draft in the digital collection is a note from someone at Morrison's publisher, Knopf: "Dear Toni, Look what I came across in the deepest darkest recesses of the bookshelf behind my door," it begins. "I thought I should send off this heirloom that should be passed down through the generations.") Their digital pedigree notwithstanding, however, a scholar who wishes to view these heirlooms must still travel to Princeton, New Jersey—perhaps as I did, first by riding Amtrak and then local commuter rail to nearby Princeton Junction and then clambering aboard the one-car "dinky" train to the campus. One then makes their way to the looming gothic façade of the Firestone Memorial Library. Only after my visitor badge had been procured, a security checkpoint passed, two flights of stairs descended, my bags stowed in a locker, a check-in at another desk, and my hands scrubbed at a plain porcelain basin could I enter the reading room with its green-shaded bankers' lamps, where most collection items (unlike Morrison's) are still wheeled out in Hollinger boxes on trolleys.

As compelling as the fire-damaged page images were, they were not what had brought me to the archives. Among the 200 linear feet and some 325 boxes of material that comprised Morrison's papers when they were first acquired in 2014 were 150 floppy disks, most of them having passed through the hands of one of her office assistants. The majority of the disks were of the 3½-inch variety, but there were 33 in the older, more cantankerous 5¼-inch format. Of these, 4 had been identified as containing files pertaining to *Beloved*. I knew that those files had been recovered using a process that involved connecting a vintage 5¼-inch drive to a modern computer using a purpose-built controller card as the hardware bridge.[2] Despite their being nearly thirty years old, the stored data had proven legible. I was also lucky in that Morrison's assistant had been using a DOS PC running Microsoft Word, so the files were saved in a familiar format, and that the diskettes themselves had been kept at a university office, thereby sparing them from the ravages of the fire. Nonetheless, when opened on the reading room workstation at which I sat, some of the electronic documents were shot through with junk code, the artifacts of formatting instructions long out of date and thus meaningless to the WordPad application the computer was outfitted with. These artifacts had the effect of scrambling certain lines of prose, usually where the page breaks in the original document had been.[3] No dust in this archive then, but instead what is sometimes called bit rot—the inevitable decay of digital information in whatever its stored form. When these glitched electronic documents were juxtaposed with the scanned images of the fire-damaged manuscripts, the screen in front of me bore witness to two very different kinds of textual trauma.

The most basic thing I wished to accomplish during my visit was to understand the relationship between the files on the four diskettes and the other *Beloved* manuscripts in the collection. Were the contents of the Word files duplicated in the page scans of hard copy materials like the one that had already arrested my attention? Or did the recovered files represent unique states of the text? And at what stage of the composition process? Questions like this are becoming increasingly commonplace as so-called born-digital materials take their place alongside manuscripts, typescripts, and printouts in archival collections. Practically speaking, there is no easy way to obtain the answer—digital files must be examined on a case-by-case basis alongside their analog counterparts in order to arrive at a complete view of the extent to which any given text's composition history is available to us through extant versions. That Morrison's paper-based materials are themselves delivered as digital page images is incidental in this regard as there is no easy way of automating searches or other comparative operations. And yet the homogeneity of the means of access in this case—both the digital photo of the damaged manuscript and the glitched text of the legacy .DOC file are each just a click away in the online finding aid—underscores the necessity of treating printed and digital materials as each mutually constitutive of the work's textual condition.

I could see from the date-stamps that all the recovered files—there are five of them across the four diskettes, each containing a different portion of the novel—had been created between July and September of 1986, the period just before the text went to Knopf for presswork.[4] The files closely resembled the so-called setting copy of the text delivered into Morrison's hands from her publisher, which she then penciled with final corrections and changes (the setting copy was not damaged in the fire and is itself accessible in its entirety at Princeton). Nonetheless, at least one of the electronic files—a document named BELOVED3.DOC— appeared to capture a minor variant state of the text not otherwise represented in the collection materials.

Readers will know that the novel ends with its title word, "Beloved," which is also the name of the two-year-old girl whom her mother, Sethe, mercy kills with a handsaw rather than allowing her to be taken by slave-catchers. In her earliest drafts, however, Morrison had instead been ending the book with "A hot thing," a phrase that appears in a monologue tendered by Beloved herself in an earlier chapter—it refers to Sethe's furnace-like love. Sometime late in the composition process, Morrison had also hand-penciled "Beloved" just above, thus making the ending read (now on two separate lines): "Beloved. / A hot thing." Morrison's editor at Knopf, Robert Gottlieb, then struck out "A hot thing," leaving "Beloved" as the final line and the final word.[5]

This was not the only consequential change effected by Gottlieb. In an essay she would publish a decade later, Morrison reflected back on the novel's editing process, drawing attention to what was to become its penultimate line, "Certainly no clamor for a kiss." She had originally written "Certainly no clamor for the join." That word—likewise resonant throughout the novel, and accompanied by a definite rather than indefinite article—was chosen by Morrison because it "connected everything together from epigraph and the difficult plot to the struggles of the characters through the process of re-membering the body and its parts, re-membering the family, the neighborhood, and our national history."[6] Gottlieb, however, felt that such an unusual word was a distraction on the last page and asked for something less "esoteric." Morrison reluctantly settled on "a kiss" instead, but she had remained uneasy about the decision: *join* may indeed have been the "wrong" word, as she would later put it, but it was also the only *right* word.[7]

And yet, despite revisiting this editorial episode at some length a decade further on, Morrison makes no mention of the removal of "a hot thing," which had remained in the closing array of lines even longer. Indeed, Morrison had continued to work with the last two lines right up until the novel went to press. She appears to have first tried inverting them, and the BELOVED3.DOC file captures the text in this unique sequence: "A hot thing. / Beloved." (Here "the join" has also not yet been changed to "a kiss.") It is not until the setting copy produced soon after to create the first proofs of the book that "a hot thing" at last disappears, *still* printed as the penultimate line (despite Gottlieb's initial cancelation) but struck out there once again with a final, decisive pencil line.

What this means is that the digital file BELOVED3.DOC most likely captures this portion of the text somewhere in between Gottlieb's editorial work (and his request for a word other than "join") and the setting copy, by which time "the join" had become "a kiss" but "a hot thing" still persisted—as best I could determine, a unique state of the text not otherwise represented in the manuscripts available at Princeton.

Associated as it is with both the strength of Sethe's love and her decision to end her daughter's life, "a hot thing" is a key phrase in any reading of *Beloved*. Its presence in the closing lines of the text throughout nearly the whole of the composition process—persisting even longer than "the join"—underscores the extent to which Morrison used it to bear the emotional weight of the novel, offset only by the title word itself. Moreover, this particular sequence of variants raises the possibility of other, less conspicuous changes elsewhere in the BELOVED3.DOC file. Why does there not appear to be any corresponding printout of it that would have been digitized for researcher access by the Princeton team? Perhaps one simply did not survive, or perhaps the file was never printed in that exact state. Regardless, it is clear that *Beloved*'s final lines remained in flux right up until the moment the book went to press, and that any complete account of its textual history would have to draw upon the evidence of the surviving digital files alongside the evidence of the surviving notes, jottings, printouts, galleys, and proofs.

This was as far as I could get in the course of a day: the determination that the contents of at least one of the electronic files appeared to be *very close to but not exactly identical to* any of the hard copy manuscript materials available to researchers as page scans.[8] Given that others of Morrison's novels in the Princeton collection are represented by born-digital materials even more extensively—for example, *Paradise* (1997)—the value of examining these files alongside other manuscript materials should be plain. Most immediately for our purposes, the ultimate incommensurability of the scanned images versus the actual digital document files is an object lesson in the non-self-identicality of the bitstream. Both forms of content, after all, were right there on the screen in front of me, presented as digital objects. But whereas the page scans of the manuscript materials are simply high-resolution photographs with little capacity for user manipulation beyond zooming or rotating or applying some stock filters, there is the potential to explore the word processing files in more diverse ways, exposing the bitstream to various kinds of automated analysis and interpretation. This difference is an outgrowth of the fact that the underlying binary code can be operationalized in very different ways depending on whether the data in question is string-based (like text) versus a pictorial bitmap. The former is searchable, reconfigurable, and potentially even executable; the latter lacks the capacity for manipulating discrete elements at a meaningful semantic level. There is thus no way to make comparisons between these two different data types short of manual collation, which is to say by reading and eyeballing the scans and the document files side by side on the screen.[9] File formats and their underlying data representations—JPEG and DOC, TIFF and TXT—create many of the conditions that enable, as well as constrain, the bibliographical encounter with the bitstream.

Manuscript archives have been receiving born-digital materials for more than two decades now, an inevitable outgrowth of the widespread shift to word processors and personal computers that swept the global North in the 1980s. When J. G. Ballard's papers arrived at the British Library in 2011, the *Guardian* opined that it was perhaps "the last solely non-digital literary archive of this stature."[10] This is not strictly true of course, but it captures the reality that an author's papers nowadays are very likely to also include digital media, everything from diskettes and CDs to hard drives and even entire computers.[11] Archivists, for their part, have become increasingly adept at the intake of such materials, at least the more common types: there are procedures and best practices for lifting the bits from different types of media and devices, for indexing their contents, for safeguarding the files on up-to-date servers, and for making copies available to researchers—although provisions for that last can be imperfect, as we have already seen. Yet whatever technical challenges they presented to the staff at the Firestone Library, Toni Morrison's diskettes (dating from the 1980s and 1990s) were still a more straightforward case than the scenario I depicted in my introduction. At Princeton, all the digital content was on physical media the archivists were able to process without regard for any conditions or terms other than those originating with Morrison herself. There were no remote servers, cloud services, or social media trails to untangle. All the files were also from easily identifiable software products in common commercial formats. Nonetheless, even in this instance, the bitstream twists and torques beneath one's fingertips, as manifest in the glitches we observed when the files were opened in WordPad.

The challenges archivists now face when confronted with the digital legacies of writers or other public figures are, of course, just a reflection of a much broader set of changes in relation to how contributions to the public sphere become part of collective memory amid the always-on torrent of the bitstream. Vint Cerf, one of the original architects of the internet and currently an executive at Google, has popularized the notion of a digital dark ages. He offers the example of presidential historian Doris Kearns Goodwin sifting through Abraham Lincoln's papers: what will her twenty-first-century counterpart have to work with, Cerf dolefully asks, invoking email, hard drives, CD-ROMs, floppy disks, and laptops at the back of a closet. "I literally mean a dark age," he concludes. "The information is gone, it's inaccessible, it's uninterpretable."[12]

Barack Obama's Blackberry and Donald Trump's Twitter feed will both constitute important sources for Goodwin or one of her successors. Both are also subject to the Presidential Records Act, as were the missing emails that came to light late in George W. Bush's second term. None of these instances have actually taken archivists unaware: conversations about so-called machine-readable or electronic records were being had at the meetings of the Society of American Archivists as far back as the 1960s.[13] By 1974, F. Gerald Ham, then president of the SAA, had warned of the digital's yawning precipice in an address entitled "The Archival Edge."[14] The challenges Ham enumerated included the exponentially increasing volume of archival records as well as the challenge of missing records—for example, telephone conversations (the address's timing with respect to the Watergate tapes is not incidental here); the sheer number of record makers in a media age, meaning archives are no longer solely a repository for the records of the state; and finally, what he termed simply "technology," including the new forms of electronic data storage emerging even then. In all of this he was to prove prescient. From family photo albums (now replaced by an Instagram account) to the National Archives, we are coming to terms with the new realities anticipated by Ham. Consider the circumstance not only of presidential historians but of anyone seeking to study most any aspect of recent history, with the profusion of digital records and data across every segment of society. The 2016 (and 2020) presidential election in the USA, Brexit in the UK, #BlackLivesMatter, #MeToo, the coronavirus pandemic . . . all these movements and events are fully and deeply integrated with the bit-streams of digital media.

This is an especially bracing set of considerations to enter into collective consciousness when we consider the *other* big questions about data now dominating public discourse: those having to do, of course, with privacy, surveillance, data mining, and algorithmic profiling in relation to what legal scholar Frank Pasquale has termed the black box society.[15] Pasquale has in mind the unprecedented opacity of the major tech corporations (and government agencies) to public oversight, and accountability. The very telephone conversations Ham used as an example of uncollectible and unquantifiable data are now routinely tracked and collected by intelligence agencies or service providers or both, as is common knowledge in the wake of Edward Snowden's revelations. Far from being fleeting and ephemeral, the reality of the internet is that a careless word (or image) is all but impossible to efface and expunge. Many now advocate for a "right to be forgotten" as a basic human right—a counterweight to the 24/7 churn of information engines that seem to collect everything, keep it indefinitely, and mine it in unspecified and unspoken ways to forge ever-evolving data profiles ramifying through all facets of an individual's life. Such data profiles are not neutral but rather, as scholars like Virginia Eubanks and Safiya Umoja Noble have shown, they are shaped by the biases and blind spots our algorithms inherit from the data scientists who compose them.[16] We thus have the specter of a digital dark ages being conjured at the very moment of widespread concern about whose digital data is being collected, how much of it is being collected, and how it can be exploited. How to account for this seeming contradiction, a simultaneous anxiety over scarcity and anxiety over abundance?

The seeming homogeneity of the bitstream—the convergence of voice, text, video, and all manner of communications channels in an underlying lingua franca of ones and zeros—is what makes "archiving" on this vast scale possible, at least in theory. But these data archives require massive investments in infrastructure, with concomitant environmental and economic impacts.[17] Take the one-million-square-foot data center the U.S. government completed for a reported $1.5 billion near Bluffdale, Utah, some twenty miles south of Salt Lake City—known officially as the Intelligence Community Comprehensive National Cybersecurity Initiative Data Center. The plans include provisions for a dedicated electrical substation designed to handle the 65-megawatt demand from, among other elements, some 60,000 tons of cooling equipment through which 1.7 million gallons of water will be pumped each day. According to computer security expert James Bamford, the facility is designed to collect and store "the complete contents of private emails, cell phone calls, and Google searches, as well as all sorts of personal data trails—parking receipts, travel itineraries, bookstore purchases, and other digital 'pocket litter.'"[18] The need to keep servers inside of temperature-controlled rooms (probably not exceeding around 68 degrees Fahrenheit in an area where daytime temperatures can approach 100 degrees Fahrenheit) and surrounding them with physical security (starting with the isolated locale itself) testifies to the interface between the bitstream and the material realities of the planet and its resources, where data is made not just of ones and zeros but also of rare earth minerals and fossil fuels. The scale of the data to be "archived" there—the magnitude of the bitstream to be wrangled—will likely be measured in "yottabytes," one yottabyte equaling one septillion bytes, a unit of measure so large that until recently there was no nomenclature for whatever the *next* highest order of magnitude might be.[19]

All of this is a long way from Toni Morrison's 360-kilobyte diskettes, small matte black squares to which handwritten labels still cling, affixed by slowly dissolving adhesives. But the strange, torqueing topographies of the bitstream made manifest in settings as dissonant as a top-secret government data facility and a university library reading room are a reflection of the same extreme forces that led Jacques Derrida, two decades after Ham, to tell an audience at the Freud Museum in London that "nothing is less reliable, nothing is less clear today than the word 'archive.'"[20] Many readers have since noted the figurative or allusive character of Derrida's use of *the* archive throughout this famous lecture to name a complex of questions related to origin, memory, patronage, and power—as opposed to providing a description of any actual institutions and repositories. Carolyn Steedman, who is one of the most careful readers of *Archive Fever*, describes Derrida's archive as "a metaphor capacious enough to encompass the whole of modern information technology, its storage, retrieval, and communication."[21] Information studies scholar Michelle Caswell expands on what is at stake in the definite article:

> For humanities scholars, "the archive" denotes a hypothetical wonderland, the "first law of what can be said, the system that governs the appearance of statements as unique events," according to Foucault, or a curious materialization of the death drive and pleasure principle according to Derrida. . . . For archival studies scholars and practicing archivists, archives—emphasis on the "s"— are collections of records, material and immaterial, analog and digital (which, from an archival studies perspective, is just another form of the material), the institutions that steward them, the places where they are physically located, and the processes that designated them "archival."[22]

Derrida's archive is thus what we might call a theory-fiction, a trope that made the "question" of the archive usable—consumable—for theory itself. Nevertheless, it is also clear that Derrida succeeded in diagnosing, at just the right moment, a fluttering anxiety born of his privileged audience's unarticulated sense that *the* archive—understood broadly as a site for memory and inscription—a site not of the past but of the present, as Derrida himself repeatedly insisted—was changing under their feet, or (better) under their fingertips. Maybe they had just accidentally sent an "E-mail" to the wrong addressee: Where *was* it, exactly? Why couldn't it be recalled?

Steedman notes that such musings were by then "commonplace";[23] indeed, the Canadian archivist Terry Cook had broached all of that and more in the context of a paper on "electronic records and paper minds" a year earlier in 1993, the same year that Donald F. McKenzie delivered his remarks on paper versus digital texts to the Bibliographical Society of London.[24] Other colorful terms were also coming into use. "Cyberspace," cyberpunk science fiction author Bruce Sterling enthused, "is the 'place' where a telephone conversation appears to occur. Not inside your actual phone, the plastic device on your desk. Not inside the other person's phone, in some other city. *The place between* the phones."[25] In the popular imagination at the time, this place between—this cyberspace—was memorably limned by William Gibson's "lines of light" and the Cartesian neon of the Disney film *TRON*.[26] Today, however, the space of cyberspace is more prosaic (measured out, as we have seen, in liquid gallons and electrical megawatts) and the *place between* is pinpointed on Google Maps (heat signatures and newly lofted power pylons registered with aerial instrumentation). There those self-same phone conversations (and much more) are collected, stored, sifted, sorted, and operationalized for the exercise of state power. (Here Derrida's etymology of the *arkhē* hits home.)

As Sterling was glossing cyberspace as a world elsewhere, the first generation of home computers was already passing into obsolescence. "New media," as Jonathan Sterne once observed, "are 'new' primarily with reference to themselves."[27] Computers, in other words, assert their novelty mainly through comparison with their own predecessors, in retail generations more foreshortened than anything the market has previously known. (The Apple II Sterling had on his desk was an ancestral relic alongside the *petit Mac* on which Derrida boasted of writing the lecture that became *Archive Fever*.) As a result, mute material reminders of previous product cycles—abruptly incompatible cords and cables, connectors and suddenly prehistoric power supplies—tend to stay with us, filling up our own worldly habitus by arrogating space in drawers and shelving and closets. Sterling wrote a manifesto, and he began cataloging obscure and obsolescent technologies. He called it the Dead Media Project.[28]

It changed the way he spoke about the digital. A decade later, in 2004, Sterling was more apt to tell his readers something like this: "Bits, digital ones and zeros, are not numbers or Platonic abstractions. They are physically real and subject to entropy, just like leaky plumbing. Bits are electrons moving through circuits, or photons in a fibre-optic pipe. Bits are laser burn marks in plastic, or iron filings stuck together with tape. Those are the weird stopgaps that we are using for heritage." Gone was talk about telephones and places in between, let alone cyberspace. In terms Friedrich Kittler would have appreciated, bits were abruptly reduced to electrons or photons in circuits and tubes. "A book, given acid-free paper and stable inks, will last for centuries in a dark dry room," Sterling continued. "Nothing created with a computer has ever enjoyed any such persistence." Bits, he recognized, required constant attention and upkeep in order to survive for even a decade or two. "The digital computer is about as old as I am," he concluded, "yet it does not have, and has never had, any archival medium." [29] An archive, he explained, is not just a pile of stuff somewhere; it requires care, attention, and ongoing and expert oversight: "Some expensively trained, salaried human being has to take responsibility and exercise control: selecting, organizing, describing, pruning the rot and encouraging new growth: and doing it forever." [30]

Archival medium is a turn of phrase worth pausing over. It remakes "the" archive as an adjective, an external quality assigned as a descriptor to something else—in this case a medium of some sort. This instrumental usage is seemingly at odds with the degree of human attention and intentionality just invoked: how can anything be inherently "archival"? In fact, it had long been a commonplace in the computer industry to refer to various storage technologies precisely as archival media. But what the industry means by this is neither an archive in Sterling and Caswell's careful and deliberate sense, nor in Derrida's more capacious one—though as we will see, it bears elements of both.

John C. Urbach, a Xerox PARC research scientist writing in 1971, is a representative spokesperson: "archival memory can be defined as being inherently expandable and stable, but inaccessible for direct operations by central processors." Urbach further glosses this by stipulating that archival memory is characterized by its "relatively slow" speed of access to stored data (as opposed to data in the main memory); the cost effectiveness per bit to be stored; and that it should be expandable "without encountering sharply defined physical limits." Such storage should, in theory, allow for the "permanent or semi-permanent" retention of data. "Classic examples of such systems," Urbach concludes, "are file cabinets full of hard copy, and conventional libraries." [31]

For Urbach and others of his time, the obvious archival medium was magnetic tape, which embodied all the above advantages: it was cheap to manufacture and voluminous (as measured by its aerial density, i.e. the literal number of bits packed into a finite physical space), and it was durable and resilient, or at least it was perceived to be. (Unbeknownst to many, magnetic tape is still integral to large-scale computing infrastructures today.)[32] But magnetic tape quickly proved no less vulnerable to entropy and "leaky plumbing," no less of a "weird stop-gap" than anything else. Already by 1973 the industry publication *Datamation* had run a feature on the "Reading of Very Old Magnetic Tape," noting that tapes more than a decade old yielded error rates as high as 20 percent due to the deterioration of the magnetic surface—bit rot in the most literal sense. "Recovery of data from very old magnetic tape is a problem that we will undoubtedly all have to face some day," its author concluded.[33]

Despite such warnings, the conceit of an archival medium in computer systems design took hold. This led many in the industry to speak easily and unselfconsciously about archives and archival storage, much as they also spoke about libraries of code or, for that matter, the "reading" and "writing" of data in "files." Wang Laboratories, the market leader in word processing for much of the 1970s, referred to its flexible and flimsy 5¼-inch floppy diskettes as "archive disks" in order to differentiate their contents from a file held in the system's main memory. The archive disk, Wang users were instructed, was where they were to go to retrieve files at a future date. Likewise, the TAR file format is in fact the Tape ARchive, first introduced in 1979 to structure data into sequences of uniform blocks with associated headers, or metadata information—an arrangement designed specifically with long reels of magnetic tape in mind. TAR, in other words, was one attempt to impose order and conformity on the bitstream.[34] Because it was initially bundled with the UNIX operating system, it is still available from the command line and it remains a popular option for packaging and sending files (often compressed as a "tar.gz," a so-called tarball), even if the files in question are never retrieved from or destined for an actual tape reel. More recently, the Web ARChive or WARC file type has similarly emerged to store document sets harvested from web servers by automated crawlers. The language of archives and the archival has been thoroughly written into computers and computing.

The Society of American Archivists defines the archival in terms of permanent value to history.[35] In computer science, however, we find archives and the archival characterized by idealized functions, intimately bound up with the capacity for copying and duplication as data is shunted from one physical address to another. Grammatically speaking, archive had become a verb, just as "text" itself eventually would too. Computing thus made the word archive (or its surrogates, like *Save*) into a command—a consignation—in ways Derrida would have appreciated. (Computing, it seems, turns everything it touches into a transitive.) The defining characteristic of an archive in the digital sense is now redundancy. Lots of Copies Keeps Stuff Safe (LOCKSS) is both a heuristic and the actual name of a consortium for the distributed institutional care of digital collections.[36]

Moreover, as archives—in Sterling and Caswell's sense of collections and institutions—now come to include artifacts like Toni Morrison's diskettes, or for that matter TAR and WARC files, there is a curious semantic doubling that ensues: those institutions become responsible for the care of artifacts that are or were in their own day *already spoken of* as archival media, or quite literally as an "archive." The media archaeologist Wolfgang Ernst would doubtless take this as confirmation of the necessity for "archiving the term *archive* itself" in relation to digital storage, out of conviction that the conceit of permanence attending the archive is incompatible with the ontology of the medium.[37]

The shift from *an* archives (as a place) or even *the* archive (as a trope) to *archiving* as an active and ongoing process had been anticipated in the archives profession by Terry Cook, who reminds us that behind the record lies the need to record, and behind the document lies a desire to document; so too, behind "the" archive lies the need, the act, the desire—perhaps even the fever—*to* archive.[38] But whereas the action verbs Cook names have hardened into nouns, "archive," by contrast—disrupted by computing and the avalanche of electronic records—has followed the reverse path and has been reanimated as active and transitive. The archiving of digital assets is best understood as a continually active *process*, requiring ongoing care, attention, and maintenance to ensure that systems remain secure, software stays up to date, connections don't deteriorate, and bits don't rot. Archivists overseeing digital collections perform what are called fixity checks for example, at set intervals using a mathematical calculus to verify that the sequence of bits comprising a given digital object has not changed, either through accident or intervention. To archive in this sense is the continuous renewal of a stance of commitment.

The work of Wendy Hui Kyong Chun is clarifying at this juncture since it allows us to see why archives as sites of active and continuous renewal are—perhaps counterintuitively—deeply compatible with the fluxes and flows of the bitstream.[39] Chun's project hinges on her having diagnosed a "conflation" between memory and storage that, as she sees it, "both underlies and undermines digital media's archival promise."[40] The archival promise that is here spoken of is the popular belief that information, once digitized, is available more or less permanently to collective recall, whether via a simple search query or else through more elite channels of access, as brokered by facilities like Bluffdale. The problem with any such promise is already familiar: namely, how easy it is to forget that when we speak of archiving or saving something digitally, we are really speaking about material media and material vulnerabilities. Tape becomes brittle, disks fail, bits *do* rot, and that which was thought safely and securely stored into memory is again imperiled. (This is the allure of the cloud, with its server farms and data warehouses we never see; absent privileged entry to the secure premises of the data center, cloud storage will never become anything so mundane as an actual medium to the consumer.) For just this same reason, it was all too easy for Claude Shannon to "forget" to label the blank (black) box at the center of his diagram, the one that encoded the tangible reality of the media on which his transmission model depended. The profiles of the anonymous low-slung buildings rising from the Utah scrub and the flimsy plastic sheaths protecting the ferrous oxide surfaces of Morrison's diskettes are *each* material shadows of that unlabeled black box.

The conceit of "storing" something in "memory" (commonplace in computer parlance) is, in Chun's account, an infelicitous and inverted usage. Memory, for Chun, is retrospective and commemorative; storage, by contrast, is forward looking. Our interest in storage is inherently subjunctive and anticipatory: we store away goods or resources for the future—the proverbial rainy day or hour of need. Only in computing do we speak of storing things in *memory*; everywhere else we would *remember* that which had been stored. Moreover, Chun notes that "memory" was introduced into computing's lexicon only with the advent of regenerative devices like mercury delay lines and Williams tubes in the mid-1940s (essentially the same cathode ray tubes that would become the basis of modern screen technology). In a Williams tube, the properties that allow electrons to "paint" a phosphorescent coating and project an image on a screen can also be used to store numbers. Such a stored value is, however, fundamentally unstable; it is constantly degenerating and so must be continually regenerated or refreshed (as much as five times per second), much as we talk about refresh rates for a CRT screen. Chun finds these details of antiquated photoelectric processes to be symptomatic of the condition of digital media at large: digital memory is *always* degenerative and in need of active regeneration. This is true both technically—in the material properties of mercury delay lines and magnetic marks on the surface of tape or disk—as well as at a macro level, in the churnings of the digital culture industry: the meme that just won't die, last year's viral video that you thought you'd never see again until someone for whom it is apparently still fresh sends it to you yet one more time. Chun derives the conceit of the "enduring ephemeral" to express a temporal as opposed to a spatial register for the digital archive.

The degenerative (and regenerative) qualities of digital memory lead Chun to the same cycles of repetition Derrida saw as symptomatic of the archive's feverish death drive.[41] Indeed, if repetition through multiplication is the essence of digital data storage, every repetition also consumes the ever-diminishing resources of the planet as the power grid expands and the heat signatures of the data centers register on the landscape. Chun's framing, however, is not ecological but is presented as a crisis of the faith, a Freudian repression born of the unique character of digital memory and its codependent cycles of rot and renewal: if digital memory depends on its host medium's ongoing and essential degeneration, it also depends on our own ongoing and active repression of those same truths.[42] The reality of digital memory is that it is *always* unfolding amid a precarious temporality that cascades like the semantic relations of the bitstream itself, data only ever given meaning by other data—or as Chun has it, "a conflation of storage with access, of memory with storage, of word [or, I would interject, icon: 🖫] with action."[43]

If there is no dust in the reading room at the Firestone Library, it is because the digital objects that enable access to the Toni Morrison collection are inured to that most mundane of material accretions. Dust is, after all, the enemy of the digital. It is the reason why microprocessors are manufactured in clean rooms by workers wearing so-called bunny suits; it is why the air in the server rooms at the very best data centers is ionized to purge airborne contaminants. For all the incontrovertible evidence of the elemental forces that attacked Morrison's papers—visible in astonishingly intimate detail in the high-resolution images—the marks of trauma and distress we see on the screen are simulacra. Indeed, at the deepest of computational levels, the images we see are reconstituted anew each and every time the files are accessed, refreshed and reassembled in Gatsbyesque fashion for us to look at with our Dutch sailors' eyes. This is an ontology in which the bitstream is constantly refreshed and renewed with each revolution of a diskette and each migration or update or patch to the server that the staff at the archives undertakes; for that matter, each new budget cycle and org plan and fire marshal's inspection and security audit; each new upgrade to infrastructure and grid, plumbing and HVAC.

Dust is anathema to the digital, but it is not unlike the stuff of the digital: barely there but everywhere, literally little tiny *bits* of matter, "the minimum recognizable entity of material transformation and circulation."[44] But the most compelling way to think about dust, as writers such as Steedman have shown, is not as the simple byproduct of deterioration and decay but rather as (literally) revolutionary and regenerative. "Dust," Steedman says, "is about circularity, the impossibility of things disappearing, or going away, or being gone."[45] The historian C. V. Wedgwood, not yet thirty years of age when her great history of the Thirty Years War was published in 1938, had understood this. "Nothing," she wrote, "seems to bridge the gap of years like the folding and unfolding of ancient letters; sometimes minute particles of sand which had long adhered in some thick down stroke where the ink had been wet detach themselves after three hundred years to blow away and join with yesterday's dust."[46]

Dusting—like archive, both noun and verb, a Janus-word that encompasses acts of both application and removal—is, as Michael Marder notes, really just the redistribution of dust, its temporary elemental dislocation: earth to air and back again, a flipping of bits.[47] (Dust *to* dust, as the burial ritual reminds us.) There is no dust in the data centers and server farms, it is true, just as there is no real lint among the digital pocket litter collected there; but in their enduring ephemerality—in the gaps between definite and indefinite articles, in the gaps between scarcity and abundance, between non-places and places, memory and storage, and above all, between zeros and ones—we find the cycles of revolution and renewal that are the ontological essence of the bitstream.

The 5¼-inch diskettes on which Morrison's files were stored would have once spun at some three hundred revolutions per minute. The platters of the hard drive on the server where their archived copies now reside spin exponentially faster—indeed, it is more likely that this server does not even have spun platters at all but is comprised of solid-state memory wherein data is stored as an electrical charge. But there are other ways in which Chun's cycles of degeneration and renewal are enacted for these precious bits of heritage ("heirlooms") that are now part of Princeton's manuscript collections. Despite the evidentiary value of labels, sleeves, and other physical accouterments of digital storage media, typical practice in archival settings such as this is to decouple the content—the files—from their material conveyors. When I ask to see the original *Beloved* diskettes, they are delivered to me in a Hollinger box, ironically the only physical items I am permitted to handle in the course of my visit. The files themselves, as we have seen, were transferred—migrated, as preservationists like to say—to a server integrated into the library's existing information architecture, where they will become the subject of regular backups, an upgrade schedule, and physical security, as well as subject to the institution's protocols for secure information handling.

But while digital files can often be lifted intact from long out-of-date storage media, and while they can be delivered as content via intranet or the internet, there is no guarantee that the files will prove readable using the software we have today. Toni Morrison's .DOC files proved only partially legible in this regard, even when accessed with a product from the same vendor. Many digital objects, once migrated from their original conveyances, persist only as so-called BLOBs, which is how preservationists refer to Binary Large OBjects—chunks of undifferentiated and functionally inaccessible digital code, structurally intact but inscrutable to whatever combinations of operating systems and applications are

3 | Four of the five 5¼-inch diskettes containing draft portions of *Beloved* at Princeton's Firestone Library. Note the handwritten information on the diskettes' labels and sleeves. Photograph by the author. By permission of the Princeton University Library, Special Collections.

now at hand. Such content is undeniably palpable and present—taking up disk space, subject to fixity checks, and perhaps even yielding metadata lodged in the header of a file. But it cannot be accessed absent more specialized interventions, whether the procurement of an equally vintage software package, emulation of the original operating system, or the use of tools to "hack" and reverse engineer the file's data structure with the goal of extracting its content and rendering it in some novel way.[48]

Even as the bitstream jumps from one physical carrier to the next, data can be accessed with fidelity if and only if an appropriately relational software regimen is available—a phenomenon I have previously termed formal materiality. But the forensic materiality—and the *reality*—of those physical carriers is also what *allows* for the interventions that leverage the bitstream into new contexts, where that regimen can be practically enacted—as is the case with a hardware bridge from a vintage floppy drive to a USB port on a modern computer, where the files can be stored, copied again at will, and finally, with sufficient resources and motivation, reconstituted and read. This accomplished, the diskettes become a mere relic, a husk set aside for the curious like me.[49]

Beloved, as any reader of it knows, is a story about memory. In a much-quoted passage, Sethe says to her daughter Denver: "Some things go. Pass on. Some things just stay. I used to think it was my rememory. You know. Some things you forget. Other things you never do. But it's not. Places, places are still there. If a house burns down, it's gone, but the place—the picture of it—stays, and not just in my rememory, but out there, in the world."[50] It is an uncanny intimation of the house fire still a half decade in Morrison's own future. But there is also the startling introduction of the word rememory as a way of naming a past trauma externalized beyond an individual consciousness, a construct that "neatly conjoins the novel's supernatural vision with its aspiration to communal epic," in the words of the critic Caroline Rody.[51] In a novel whose title character is a ghost, rememory in essence turns the entire landscape into a haunting, with any given place or object harboring the potential for being revealed as the lingering residue of past events. Sethe explains as much to Denver: "The picture is still there and what's more, if you go there—you who never was there—if you go there and stand in the place where it was, it will happen again; it will be there, waiting for you."[52] Marisa Parham astutely notes the layers of superimposed slippages in this key passage, first as memory becomes spatial as much as temporal, but then also as the mode of second person address—*you*—is revealed as itself a subject conditioned and created by impressed memory. "The problem," explains Parham, "is not that this memory has agency, is waiting for you, but that there was in fact no you prior to this encounter. What at first seems a slip between time and place is thus revealed as a displacement, as you are made to know that that which constitutes you comes from elsewhere, and that it will come with or without your consent."[53]

Rememory subordinates time to the dilation of those traumas that "just stay," like the scars of a whipping on Sethe's back in the shape of a chokecherry tree. Morrison's neologism also complicates Chun's etymology of the root word memory, which Chun locates in the Sanskrit for *martyr*; the stutter of rememory seems closer to something like that which is "stored" in Chun's account: "*storage* usually refers to something physical or substantial, as well as to its physical location," she states.[54] Elsewhere Chun suggests that the infelicitous inversion of storage and memory in the technical lexicon "hardens information—turning it from a measure of possibility into a 'thing' "[55]—possibly like the binary large objects glossed above. If, as Chun suggests, "memory" was grafted into the language of computing as a lexical cover for the material realities of actual storage technologies that permit no true past—only a kind of endlessly and precariously renewed perpetual present—then Morrison's rememory becomes its own form of enduring ephemeral, a palpable "picture" conjoined (like Sethe's scars) with indelible trauma. In short, rememory (slipping and superimposed in the manner articulated by Parham) would seem to name the very infelicity or conflation that Chun exposes as at the heart of our contemporary experience of the digital archive and its rupturing of the categories of past, present, and future.[56] Scholars of Black memory such as Saidiya Hartman would, I think, perceive the same infelicity as Chun, the same arrest and arrogation of temporal flow as integral not just to the digital archive but to *all* archives as political and ideological projections of the colonial violence of whiteness, power, and the state.[57]

Juxtaposing the lived experience of chattel slavery with the intricacies of modern information technology may seem abrupt, even infelicitous (or worse) in its own right.[58] But the juxtaposition is compelled, I would want to argue, by the textual condition of *Beloved*'s scorched and scarred manuscript pages, consigned as they now are to the bitstream along with the digital files extracted from the author's disks. If computer "memory" in Chun's account is a pastness perpetually and oxymoronically wrenched into some proleptic future through the functional repression of the material realities of data storage, then rememory would seem to name something very similar.[59] *Some things just stay.* The digital files that I looked at, not unlike one of Sethe's "pictures," are there, enduring *and* ephemeral, and if *you* go to Princeton they will be there and they will "happen" again.

And yet, perhaps when you go, the desktop software will have been upgraded and the glitched passages that confounded me will now render properly. Perhaps the monitor will have an even higher resolution, or its white point and gamma settings will be a little off that day and nothing will look quite as it should. Perhaps the reading room will be closed for renovation, or for public health because of a pandemic. Perhaps you will wear earbuds as you work (I did not); perhaps it will be fair outside instead of overcast ("the rest is weather," as Morrison says of what remains after Beloved's ghost is gone).[60] And so on. The bitstream is never truly self-identical.[61] It is worth recalling too that a given sequence of bits has no one essential meaning. Interpretation (itself a term of art in computing) is *always* present in the act of "reading" a digital file. The bitstream is as irreducibly relational in its potential for rendering as it is relentlessly linear in the logic of computation. The imperfect attempts of desktop software to display the legacy files from Morrison's diskettes is one reminder of that relationality, those portions of the files encoded as plain ASCII seamlessly reproduced, while more idiosyncratic content—formatting codes and such—surrender to the contingencies of their binary pedigree. Just as the fire that consumed Morrison's home attacked the pages of her manuscripts—damaging some beyond saving—the flickering recursions of the bitstream disrupt the cycle of the archive, past to present and back to future perfect storage once again. The difference, though, is that the immolated edges of a manuscript are gone forever, carbonized and vaporized in a flash; the bitstream, if fixity and integrity are maintained, awaits only the imposition of the appropriate formal regimen to cauterize its internal cascade of relational disarray and rememory its pixels all anew.

Where Bruce Sterling once went looking for dead media, Chun speaks of the digital as reanimated, which is to say undead. She means that given the interaction—conflation—between storage and memory and the reciprocating cycles of retrieval and access that visit themselves upon even the most mundane matter on our screens, nothing that is digital is ever truly present and nothing may be ever truly gone.[62] This is no less true of the digital files on Morrison's diskettes, uncannily reanimated at the behest of a mouse click, than it is the unfathomably vast data troves in the server array now embedded in the Utah scrub. Ghosts, we may intimate, re-member themselves amid the clamor of all those carefully cooled machines. But ghosts are also, as *Beloved* teaches us, born and banished by the hot thing of a mother's love. The archive, as Derrida once lectured, gathers. But it is dust that joins.

2 | The Poetics of Macintosh

The year 1987, when *Beloved* was published, was also the year of the tenth anniversary issue of the *New England Review / Bread Loaf Quarterly*. Like other issues of the prestige literary journal, this one featured a special themed section. And on this landmark occasion, the theme chosen by the editors was "The Writer and the Computer." Responsibility for arranging the selections was given to William H. Dickey, a San Francisco poet who had nearly a dozen well-received books and chapbooks to his name.

As Dickey remarks in his introduction to the issue, computers—and especially word processors—had become a staple of shop talk wherever writers gathered.[1] Since the beginning of the decade, writers of all stripes—from genre fiction to *belles lettres*—had been making their acquaintance with the glowing glass screens. But there was hardly universal enthusiasm. "Word processing is erasing literature," Gore Vidal grumped in the *New York Review of Books*, even as many of his contemporaries evangelized the novelty of being able to delete and insert at their slightest whim.[2] (Still others, like Toni Morrison, saw the advantage but delegated word processing to their assistants.) Ironically, the most widely read piece from the *NER/BLQ* issue turned out to be Wendell Berry's "Why I Am Not Going to Buy a Computer," subsequently reprinted in *Harper's*.[3] Dickey himself, who had been using computers for several years already, was more measured and thoughtful in his assessment of the technology, wondering what it might do to writing itself. "Do we think differently about what we are writing if we are writing it with a reed pen or a pen delicately whittled from the pinion of a goose, or a steel pen manufactured in exact and unalterable replication in Manchester," he mused. "Do we *feel* differently, is the stance and poise of our physical relationship to our work changed, and if it is, does that change also affect the nature and forms of our ideas?"[4]

The year 1987 also happened to be when Apple released its Macintosh II and Macintosh SE computers. These were the next generation of Macintosh products, clearly descended from the original Mac of three years prior—the SE retained its diminutive appliance-like appearance—but with hardware upgrades to suit the current marketplace. Both of the new models had expansion slots (SE stood for System Expansion), which allowed users to customize their machines with the addition of circuit cards for a color display, networking capabilities, DOS compatibility, and more. This was a break from prior Macintosh product design, whose philosophy had willfully foreclosed any possibility of customization.[5]

With its internal hard drive (another first for Macintosh), the SE was intended as an all-around computer for home and business. William Dickey, born in 1928, would become the owner of one in 1988 at the age of sixty. So too would Kamau Brathwaite, a Barbados-born poet just two years younger than Dickey who encountered the Macintosh during a residency at Harvard in 1988. Brathwaite, himself a seasoned computer user, was no less thoughtful about what they were doing to his writing; indeed, computers—and specifically the Macintosh SE and an accompanying Apple StyleWriter printer—became an integral part of his poetics and personal mythos.

This chapter provides an opportunity to consider the careers of two very different writers, both of whom were using the same type of Macintosh computer at exactly the same time. Dickey, though never exactly famous, had impeccable establishment credentials—his first book, written under John Berryman's tutelage at Iowa, had been selected by W. H. Auden for the Yale Younger Poets in 1959 (among his competitors that year: Sylvia Plath). Brathwaite, by contrast, was an outsider, a liminal figure working in a Caribbean-English idiolect he termed nation language. Yet both of them were struck by the fluid and aleatory nature of writing on the Macintosh: "writing with light" was the phrase Brathwaite would use over and over again. Both were also struck by the seeming orality of composing on the screen, turning poems into events that could be manipulated in space and even time. And both used the capabilities of the Macintosh platform to innovate, Dickey teaching himself a powerful piece of software known as HyperCard whereas Brathwaite used the Mac's layout and font design capabilities (what was newly termed "desktop publishing") to attempt to garner complete creative control over the design of his books, a move that would create friction between him and his publishers.

Despite these similarities, however, their stories have very different outcomes. Dickey died of complications from HIV in 1994. His Hyper-Card poetry would remain unpublished and mostly unread for the next two and a half decades. Brathwaite's output from his Macintosh has been prodigious in the interim, but the end product of his digital experimentation was always paper. His poetry has been published by a number of trade, university, and small presses, but we have no entrée into the interior of his Macintosh and we know relatively little about how he actually composed and executed the work—notwithstanding considerable critical commentary on what is typically termed his "signature" or "trademark" Sycorax Video Style. This lacuna is eerily in keeping with the lifelong concern for archives and memory that haunted Brathwaite until his death—in 2020—at the age of almost ninety.

My purpose in what follows is not to provide a comprehensive introduction to the rich and multivalent poetics of either Dickey or Brathwaite but rather to offer a meditation of sorts on their literary legacies as they descend to us through the interleaved mediations of software and paper, published and unpublished work, and the interventions of certain key individuals. The stories I have to tell in this chapter should be read for the contours they create, contours that allow us to see how history, memory, and media serve to shape and channel the flow of the bit-stream.

The Apple Macintosh was the first glimpse many would have of what now seems universal: using a mouse to point and click at icons on a screen organized around office metaphors like a desktop, filing cabinets, folders, and a wastebasket. It debuted with a 1984 Super Bowl XVIII commercial that has since become iconic in its own right, a commercial that, like Macintosh itself, sought to transform people's ideas about what computing could be. While IBM was repurposing Charlie Chaplin's vaudeville tramp in magazine and television ads for PC and PCjr, Apple hired Ridley Scott fresh from the set of *Blade Runner* (1982). He reprised the film's noir aesthetic to give viewers a dystopian backdrop for ordered ranks of empty-eyed carceral figures. On a screen in front of them floated the face of a Big Brother oppressor meant to personify Big

Blue, as IBM was known in the industry. Enter an athletic woman swinging a sledge hammer—Macintosh incarnate, as the stylized rendition of the product on her tank-top made clear. The sixty-second spot ends with her hurling the hammer through the image of the Orwellian talking head haranguing the stupefied masses, shattering the oversized screen. The famous final text and voice-over: "On January 24th, Apple Computer will introduce Macintosh. And you'll see why 1984 won't be like '1984.'"[6]

The reality of Macintosh, however, proved more quotidian. It shipped with just two programs, MacWrite and MacPaint. MacWrite, the word processor, was found to be unable to load or save documents of more than about eight pages in length and was widely panned. But MacPaint was a revelation. Written by a young programmer named Bill Atkinson, the key to it was the Macintosh's bitmapped screen, technology that had been pioneered at Xerox PARC more than a decade earlier with a computer called the Alto. The Alto, with its own bitmapped display, a mouse, and other features Xerox never imagined there would be any consumer interest in (!), was a legend, but only insiders—and visitors to PARC, of which Steve Jobs was famously one—had ever seen it.[7] A bitmap turned a computer monitor into a kind of matrix wherein each Cartesian point on the screen—each bit or "pixel"—corresponded to a specific addressable location in memory, meaning it could be turned on or off (and also assigned color values). At a high enough resolution, the Mac could offer graphics, which, if not quite photorealistic, were still better than anything else on the market. More to the point, images could be easily edited and manipulated, just as people had quickly become accustomed to doing with words in a word processor. MacPaint introduced this capability to the masses, effectively giving every new Mac user their own "picture processor."

Meanwhile, MacWrite, for all its limitations, put sophisticated desktop typography at users' fingertips for the first time. Fonts on the Mac's bitmapped screen were proportional, meaning that they took up variable amounts of horizontal space on the screen—an uppercase W and a lowercase l, for example, each claimed space in proportion to their actual width, allowing for kerning, ligatures, and other effects. The Mac shipped with a dozen proportional fonts, most of them created by the artist Susan Kare, who had also designed its memorable palette of desktop icons. And like text in MacWrite or images in MacPaint, fonts could be edited and indeed fashioned from scratch on the Macintosh with comparative ease. Owing to early programs with names like Fontastic, there were soon dozens and then hundreds of such fonts in circulation; designers like Zuzana Licko and Rudy VanderLans (who co-founded *Émigré* magazine) crafted a whole typographic aesthetic around the Macintosh, as would, just a few years later, Kamau Brathwaite. (This could, of course, be easily overdone; the journalist Gay Talese once likened the experience of choosing fonts in MacWrite to a child asked to choose among flavors in an ice cream shop.)[8] Taken together, MacWrite and MacPaint—and other Mac-specific programs that would soon follow, like Aldus PageMaker and Adobe Illustrator—blurred the lines between words and images.

None of this happened by chance. Steve Jobs had learned what he knew about art and typography during an abortive stint as an undergraduate at Reed College in Portland, Oregon. Calligraphy had been introduced to the curriculum at Reed in 1949 by an English professor and hand-press printer named Lloyd J. Reynolds. Owing to Reed's proximity to the Bay Area, Reynolds would get to teach and influence a number of undergraduates who went on to careers in the graphic arts, eventually working for companies like Adobe and Apple: Charles Bigelow, Kris Holmes, and Sumner Stone all among them.[9]

Reynolds had retired by the time Jobs arrived in 1972, but his successor, a calligrapher and Trappist monk named Robert Palladino, continued to teach the graphic arts curriculum until his own retirement. These would be the classes Jobs would audit, an episode that has since become part of Macintosh lore. As Jobs tells it:

> Throughout the campus every poster, every label on every drawer, was beautifully hand calligraphed. Because I had dropped out and didn't have to take the normal classes, I decided to take a calligraphy class to learn how to do this. I learned about serif and sans serif typefaces, about varying the amount of space between different letter combinations, about what makes great typography great. It was beautiful, historical, artistically subtle in a way that science can't capture, and I found it fascinating.
>
> None of this had even a hope of any practical application in my life. But 10 years later, when we were designing the first Macintosh

computer, it all came back to me. And we designed it all into the Mac. It was the first computer with beautiful typography. If I had never dropped in on that single course in college, the Mac would have never had multiple typefaces or proportionally spaced fonts.[10]

Alongside the future designers and typographers, Lloyd Reynolds's students also included a number of undergraduates who would go on to become notable poets, Gary Snyder and Philip Whalen perhaps the most prominent. Also among them was a poet who would graduate in 1951 and whose first book would be selected for the Yale Younger Poets, thus launching his career. In 1966, that same poet (now well established) contributed sixteen lines in quatrains to a festschrift for his friend and one-time teacher. Called "A Fine Italian Hand" for the italic script Reynolds had taught him, they began:

If I must take up the old British fountain-pen
Again, and make my blue letters move in order
To the Italian pattern a calligrapher taught me
It is because, against the world's disorder

So little else counts. [. . .][11]

And of course, as we have seen, in one of the overlapping circular patterns that so fascinated him as a poet, William H. Dickey was eventually to own one of his fellow Reedie's calligraphically inspired computers.

Though his purchase of a Macintosh was still at least a year away when he was asked to edit the Computers and Writing issue of *New England Review / Bread Loaf Quarterly*, Dickey was already thinking in sophisticated terms about the implications of electronic composition. Indeed, we have seen that he well-remembered that fountain pen and its patterns, moving "in order . . . against the world's disorder." Movement had become a preoccupation of his poetics, and even the most basic word processors granted him a degree of freedom he would have otherwise thought impossible. Elsewhere, he observed: "No one who has worked with students composing poems on sheets of paper, within the boundaries of the persistently defining rectangle, can be unaware of the extent to which the order in which lines are placed on a page becomes an authority, even a tyranny, and how difficult it is to shift them once their first relationship has been established."[12] But commenting on his own poems in the *NER/BLQ* issue (individual words or pairs of words arranged amid large expanses of white space that he compared to both musical monody and Chinese painting), he writes: "Because these elements can be moved, repositioned with respect to one another with such ease on a computer screen, it's tempting to ask what different kinds of relationships can be encouraged among them."[13] He next asks: "What would a book be without pages? How could we begin to define one?"[14] Shortly thereafter a new software package, bundled and released with his Macintosh SE, would provide him with an answer.

Instantly lauded as transformational, HyperCard was the brainchild of the same Bill Atkinson who had programmed MacPaint. Like that earlier application, HyperCard seemed to go to the essence of what made Macintosh different—that is, why one bought a Mac at all, as opposed to an IBM PC or even another graphically capable computer like the Commodore Amiga. HyperCard relied on two central metaphors: the card and the stack. In its original implementation, once the program was launched a card would consume the whole of the screen (what we would today refer to as full-screen mode), in essence providing an entirely different interface, one that was organized not around office paraphernalia but rather cards—index or rolodex cards perhaps, but playing cards as well. They were sorted and arranged in "stacks," which was the other governing metaphor. One could move through a stack sequentially, as though flipping through a filing box or deck, but that was only the beginning. Cards could also have buttons that enabled all sorts of lateral connections between them, forming nets or webs; moreover, the cards could serve as supports for graphics and audio effects. A built-in programming language called HyperTalk added the potential for even richer kinds of interactions, including conditional and timed effects. (Because of this capability, the prototype of the bestselling computer game *Myst* [1991] was written in HyperCard.)[15] The opening page of Apple's own documentation hardly did Atkinson's vision justice: "Use [HyperCard] to look for and store information—words, charts, pictures, digitized photographs—about any subject that suits you," the manual invited in unassuming prose.[16] Douglas Adams, the bestselling science fiction author who was a Mac evangelist, put it rather more dramatically. "I think it occupies the same niche in the evolution of software as human beings do in the evolution of life," he said of HyperCard in the pages of *MacUser* magazine.[17]

Like MacWrite and MacPaint before it, HyperCard would have come pre-installed on Dickey's Macintosh. That Dickey would spot it was inevitable: its desktop icon was a stack of cards with a hand gripping a one-pixel-wide stylus poised atop them. Not exactly a fountain pen cut from British steel perhaps, but still: irresistible. The moment he clicked, Dickey would have found his heretofore notional "book without pages" literalized as a card stack, an open, unbound structure on the screen in front of him.

Dickey was to produce, to various states of completion, fourteen different compositions in HyperCard between 1988 and his death in 1994. He called them HyperPoems, and (with one exception to which I will return) none was published until two and a half decades after his death. How then do these bitstreams descend to us? In one sense the answer is mundane, involving relationships and circumstances I will summarize. On the other hand, though, the fraught transmission history of the Hyper-Poems offers a cautionary tale for the future of digital literary heritage. Dickey was not exactly a household name, it is true; but few enough poets are these days, and Dickey had enjoyed a notable and successful career by any measure. The HyperCard work unfolded in the midst of his last major creative phase and also coincided with the HIV diagnosis that eventually took his life. The poems themselves address themes characteristic of his work—history and mythology, as well as memory, sexuality, the wasteland of the modern world, and (over and under all of it) love and death—but they also represent an important progression of his poetics, one with clear roots in the ideas about poetry he had forged through decades of mindfulness about the craft. As his partner and literary executor Leonard Sanazaro noted, the "breaking down and diminishment of expected literary patterns is what fascinated and occupied Dickey during the latter portion of his artistic development."[18]

Sometimes specific words or ideas are present in common between his last published poems and the HyperPoems. For example, the closing lines from "The Education of Desire," a multipart work in his final collection of the same name (published posthumously):

4 & 5 | Screens from William Dickey's "Throats of Birds" and "Accomplished Night," both as rendered in the online emulator at the Internet Archive. Screenshots by the author from https://archive.org/details/william_dickey_hyperpoems _volume_1 and https://archive.org/details/william_dickey _hyperpoems_volume_2.

violent and singing
on the empty road
someone's arriving

the white light
cherishing his step
and his naked stare.[19]

And then these lines, from the HyperPoem entitled "Volcano":

The groups of visitors stood frozen, a flash
of white light catching and bleaching them
at the end of the Street of Tombs. The
priests searched them while they were
yet paralyzed, taking their billfolds and
purses and shelling them, until the ground
was littered with everything designed to
remember. In the end, all that was
wanted for tribute to the dead, all that
was not restored, was their names.

Here we see literal duplication of a "white light" as well as overlap in the surrounding imagery of a desolate thoroughfare, nakedness, identity stripped bare, and the end of a journey or pilgrimage. More than any express intent to place the two poems in dialogue with one another, I suspect the significance of their common elements lies in the degree to which they combine to testify to the preoccupations of Dickey's lyric imagination at the time. Put simply, the HyperPoems demand to be read as an essential and integral part of his oeuvre.

Encountering them today, it may be difficult to appreciate just how liberating the form would have been for Dickey. Though the graphics became more sophisticated as he gained confidence with the program, they initially tended to resemble clip art (and indeed, they often were)—as is the case with "Heresy" or "Fours," for example. Audio was likewise rudimentary by today's standards, stock sound effects and chiptune sequences. And yet the bitmapped screen of the Macintosh, which allowed text and image to be manipulated more or less seamlessly and in tandem, was a revelation to Dickey, unlike anything he had previously worked with. He compared the medium to Walt Disney animations as well as to illuminated manuscripts but notes that with HyperCard almost anyone "with access to a particular, and reasonably inexpensive, computer" is thus empowered.[20]

Still, HyperCard relied on a palette of tools and features, each of which had to be mastered to create the desired effect on the screen. Lassos and brushes and buckets and spray paint and pencils and erasers— Dickey experimented with them all. Perhaps most important to him, however, were the structural possibilities of the software. Transitions from one card to another took the form of a variety of cuts, fades, slides, dissolves, and swoops. Stacks could become loops and mandalas, forking paths and labyrinths. The so-called buttons embedded in the cards allowed him to sculpt patterns of repetition and difference, sometimes deliberately forcing a reader to reread, other times creating the illusion of sameness only to have the composition reveal itself anew. ("Zenobia, Queen of Palmyra" is perhaps the most accomplished in this regard.) Readers could not always be sure what the full extent of their choices (or agency) actually was. Sometimes, for example, Dickey would deliberately hide buttons in the cards, nestling them in graphics or otherwise rendering them invisible; other times, effects were random and aleatory. All these features fundamentally changed Dickey's thinking about the possibilities of poetry, moving him away from his earlier preoccupations with the differences between Manchester fountain pens and hollow reeds and toward what we would nowadays think of as time-based media. The poem became something more like a compositional score, a framework for experience.

He says this explicitly in an essay published in 1991: "As soon as we move away from textual and graphical elements in the poem, as soon as we introduce such elements as randomization, or sound, or animation, we have arrived at a work of art for which the page is no longer an adequate representation; at best the page can provide a kind of vocal or orchestral score for the poem, and even there its nature will be limiting and misleading."[21] It's a more telling claim than it might first appear, for one can also read it as anticipating the practical problems involved in publishing and distributing the HyperPoems in their original digital format—a preemptive strike against their being relegated to the flatland of print, as seemed necessary for poetry to circulate. A page later, he raises the possibility of publishing his work on disk, or else by "computer bulletin boards," samizdat fashion, "from one viewer to another" ("viewers," he notes, may also choose to "extend and vary" the work in the manner of Wallace Stevens improvising on a theme by William Carlos Williams).[22] As we will soon see, these anxieties around publication were to prove warranted.

The HyperPoems also took Dickey elsewhere his other writing did not go. Several can be described as erotica, lyrically and graphically explicit testaments to past lovers. Here too, Dickey exploited his medium: to progress further in a poem called "Accomplished Night," for example, one clicks on the head of a penis. To read, the reader must also touch. More than any one gesture, though, the novel environment of the computer may have afforded Dickey a kind of freedom conventional publication did not. Indeed, for many writers at the time, using a computer had a kind of intimacy or confessional quality that the typewriter or notebook, if only because of their long familiarity, lacked. The screen may thus have seemed to Dickey a kind of heterotopia. Regardless, these works are unique documents of gay life in San Francisco during a particularly calamitous period. They are also some of his most technically and formally accomplished, and as such are essential to any appreciation of Dickey's legacy and oeuvre.

Dickey died on May 3, 1994, at a Kaiser Permanente facility in San Francisco at sixty-five years of age. Later that same year his literary executor—Leonard Sanazaro, himself since deceased—allowed a mutual acquaintance, a writer named Deena Larsen, access to Dickey's Macintosh. Larsen was (and is) a well-known figure in electronic fiction and poetry writing, having established herself as what we might call a community organizer as well as a prolific contributor in her own right. She and Dickey had begun a correspondence several years prior, with Larsen writing a portion of her master's thesis at the University of Colorado Boulder on the HyperPoems. "So as far as I know you may go down in history as the first person to engage in explication of a hyperpoem," Dickey communicated to her. "I guess we could hardly use the standard old phrase *explication de text* for it," he added, "and *explication de multimedia* sounds pretty clumsy."[23]

With Sanazaro's permission, Larsen copied Dickey's working files from his computer, a Macintosh Centris 650 (Quadra), which he had upgraded to not long before his death. Larsen and Sanazaro then began preparing the poetry for posthumous publication with Eastgate Systems, a Massachusetts company that functioned as an amalgam of a high-tech start-up and a small literary press and which was publishing a growing and influential canon of hypertext writing. Since many of the HyperPoems were still rough and unfinished at a technical level, the process involved substantial editorial intervention on Larsen's part: "Steering between the syclla of readability and the charybdis of keeping the work intact led to some restless moments and compromises," she notes, the details of which I've written about elsewhere.[24] (Larsen describes fixing buttons, restoring broken connections, touching up graphics, and finishing up bits of code, raising a host of textual criticism questions about copy-text, intentionality, and accidental versus substantive variants.) There were to be two "volumes" from Eastgate, both distributed on diskettes inside one of their characteristic cardboard folios and with the set entitled the *Complete Electronic Poems of William Dickey*. (The erotica would have been on the second disk.) Publishing a major body of work from a poet of Dickey's stature would have been a literary coup for Eastgate; and yet, for reasons that remain murky, the *Complete Electronic Poems* never appeared. Eastgate further had plans to issue three of Dickey's compositions as a kind of preview in its in-house little magazine, the *Eastgate Quarterly Review of Hypertext*, but that never happened either.

The reasons would not have been technical: Eastgate had ample experience of publishing HyperCard stacks on disk, just as Dickey had once foreseen.[25] Nor would they have been editorial—Larsen's work had been completed. Whatever the explanation, the consequences cannot be overstated. Absent formal publication, the HyperPoems never entered into organized channels for criticism or review and for all intents and purposes became an uncharted part of Dickey's literary legacy. (There is no mention of them in his *New York Times* obituary, for example.) In 2003, Nick Montfort and Noah Wardrip-Fruin published four of the HyperPoems (including the three originally mooted for the *Eastgate Quarterly Review*) on a CD-ROM included as a supplement to the *New*

Media Reader from the MIT Press.[26] But it does not appear to have resulted in much wider recognition for the work, and certainly it failed to reach audiences not already predisposed (or compelled) to buy a big textbook about digital media.[27]

Dickey's literary papers are at his alma mater, Reed College. The collection there includes 3½-inch Macintosh diskettes, as well as 5¼-inch floppies from his first computer; the finding aid suggests at least some of the HyperCard work is present. Unlike Morrison's papers at Princeton, however, there appears to be no particular provision for patron access to the born-digital holdings. Meanwhile, however, Deena Larsen had gifted her own literary papers to the University of Maryland, where I am based. These became my route into discovering Dickey, through two essential items. First, there are the original 3½-inch diskettes she used to copy the files from Dickey's computer. There are thirteen of these (many of them are installation disks for commercial software that Larsen had repurposed on the spot) in a small cardboard box marked with the handwritten label "Dickey's Original." Second, there is the iBook laptop Larsen used to prepare the work for publication with Eastgate. The hard drive includes folders with all the working files from that project, including as well unpublished introductions to the work by both Larsen and Sanazaro.[28]

Apple ceased distribution of HyperCard in 2004, and neither the program's authoring environment nor the reader for viewing stacks are compatible with today's OS X operating system. Fortunately, I have a Macintosh SE of my own that I can use to run the original diskettes straight from Larsen's box, a solution that depends on my situation at Maryland. When I insert them, I see Dickey's HyperPoems just as he and Larsen would have—the same hardware, same operating system and software, very likely even the same sounds from inside the machine itself, the same odor of plastic polymers in the internal heat of the case. The bitstream sometimes really does seem to torque and transcend time— a rememory, we called it earlier. This is hardly sound archival practice though, as it places additional stress on the diskettes and risks compromising their precious data.

Larsen's laptop, meanwhile, is likewise still in working order, but the power cord is frayed in an alarming way, the hard drive makes foreboding noises, and the whole system is prone to freezing. The best solution would seem to be to image the diskettes using an exacting copy process, producing virtual surrogates of the original media, which I can then employ in a Macintosh emulator (an emulator, as we have seen, is a piece of software that computationally duplicates the behavior of some other hardware or software, rendering what is in essence a digital facsimile). In order to do so, however, I first have to load a copy of Apple's System 7 boot disk into my emulator, and then a virtualized copy of HyperCard itself; I can then load one of the virtualized disks into my virtualized HyperCard installation (running on my virtualized System 7 Macintosh), and select a poem such as "Volcano"—only to find myself confronted, when I do, with the following error message.

These fonts are missing from your system:

Courier 9,12
Geneva 12,14
Palatino 10,12,14,18,24
Helvetica 18,24

For text to display correctly in the stacks, make sure you have installed the fonts included with HyperCard.

To view the poem as Dickey truly intended, then, I will also have to locate virtualized instances of all the missing fonts and add them to my now-teetering tower of reanimated bitstreams.

All these details—from outmoded and unsupported software to the precarities of emulation, and from frayed power cords to missing fonts—are familiar concerns to digital preservationists, all contributing to the specter of bit rot as much or more as the actual physical deterioration of data on media. And yet, it is these same frail leavings and remains—the hard drive on a laptop that still works years past its shelf life, a used Macintosh purchased on an internet auction site, a box of diskettes full of copied files—that allow us to come to grips with the bitstream in the material, haptic way necessary to stage interventions to rejuvenate it, if only for a time. Computers are not archival media, but the bitstream owes whatever persistence it has to the material idiosyncrasies of a wide variety of more or less resilient surfaces, conductors, and conveyances, all of them the essential prerequisites for the maintenance of the enduring ephemeral.

Several years after my initial encounter with Dickey's poetry in the collection materials at Maryland, another potential solution emerged. Emulators have become increasingly capable of being run directly online. One commonplace digital preservation scenario imagines users able to configure their own literally virtual machine—hardware, software, and operating system—from a series of cloud-based resources.[29] Emulation can even be accessed from within an ordinary web browser, a working recreation of some piece of obsolescent hardware embedded much like a video clip in the surrounding page. The Internet Archive has pioneered this approach in its software collections—such that an executable emulation of an Apple II program becomes simply another form of media content accessible to the twenty-first-century viewer. (The emulation, incidentally, may run on a phone as easily as a desktop computer.) Working with Dickey's literary executor and Deena Larsen and an emulation expert, I arranged for copies of the HyperPoems to be uploaded to the Internet Archive in the summer of 2020. JavaScript-based software running on the servers there will torque the bitstreams of the poems into a simulacrum of the form they would have once assumed on the Macintosh computer for which they were intended.[30] As a result, users can at last read Dickey's HyperPoems in their original format simply by accessing them with their web browser—the closing of a loop some two and a half decades after the poems were supposed to have been published.

But the bitstream is never truly self-identical. Jerome McGann has spent a lifetime instructing us in the ways that every literary text, indeed every *text*, descends to us in multiple material forms with "multiple, often contradictory meanings that *are a function of those material forms.*" He compares, for example, the text of Byron's *Don Juan* as it appeared in 1819 in both "a handsome quarto on good rag paper" and numerous pirated editions in "cheap duodecimos."[31] One of those texts was "a poem of remarkable elegance and wit, an ornament for those who could afford to buy the guinea quarto edition," McGann observes; the other, however, was "a poisonous work, pandering to depraved imaginations." These precepts are no less true when the text in question is born-digital, and even—or especially—when the bitstream creates its eerie, Klein bottle-like illusions of originality and simultaneity. Dickey's digital poetry means one thing to us when we sit sequestered amid the detritus of obsolescent tech, teasing the cranky HyperCard stacks to the surface of the screen by sending electrons coursing through the circuits of decades-old hardware; it means something else in samizdat circulation among a small circle of enthusiasts; and it means something *else* when virtualized through the abstractions of emulation at the Internet Archive, reliant upon a technology that was still only in its infancy when Dickey died in 1994.

In the foreword to *The Education of Desire*, Dickey's final, posthumous volume of poetry issued in 1996, W. D. Snodgrass ventures, "The most important point is that these poems, written at the end of his life and with his death of AIDS clearly in sight, are a young man's poems."[32] This proposition lends a pleasing circularity to Dickey's career, a shaping he would have appreciated given his oft-stated fascination with mandala-like patterns and loops—formal qualities that manifested themselves explicitly in the navigational structures of the HyperPoems. And yet Snodgrass's foreword, generous though it is, makes no mention of the experiments in digital composition that had unfolded contemporaneously with many of the poems included in that volume. The only trace of their existence is an unintentional counterfactual in the last sentence of the author's note that is the final item in the book, except for its Library of Congress catalog data: "The *Complete Electronic Poems of William Dickey* has recently been published by Eastgate Systems" is how the note concludes.[33] The past tense suggests that whoever prepared the text regarded the publication of the HyperPoems as a *fait accompli*. The truth, we have seen, was to remain otherwise, for some two and a half decades. And yet Dickey, who so cherished circular figures and patterns, seems to have anticipated his eventual digital revival. As he writes in "Volcano":

This is my letter to you. What I had
not thought to say, but to fold, as
we fold away the evening or the
butterflies, carefully, in the pattern
of stiff brocade, creasing it, making
the folds lie sharp and exact that
are only meant to crumble and
break from their own weight, years
later, when the person is opened,

when what is left is a breath of
voice, rising transparently, the logic
behind the perfume, all of what
once was sense stinging a little at
range beyond range of air.

For all the hype that attended its launch, sales of the original Macintosh (which was priced at $2,495) soon slumped. The problems with MacWrite were only the beginning. The Mac's 9-inch monochrome screen was pinched and cramped by the market's standards. Even more significantly, the first Mac shipped with a mere 128K of RAM memory; and it had no cooling fan because Jobs didn't like the noise. This was a combination that could slow the machine to a crawl. Finally, there was just a single built-in 3½-inch disk drive. To move files from one disk to another, one had to swap disks back and forth, in and out of the same drive, repeatedly. The process was "akin to using a thimble to transfer water from one bucket to another."[34] Reviewers were quick to notice all these deficiencies, and so were consumers. Already losing ground to IBM and other competitors, with so much invested in Macintosh Apple's future was in jeopardy. When its shareholders noticed too a boardroom showdown ensued and Jobs was famously forced from the company.

But Macintosh couldn't simply be abandoned. Some of its problems were relatively easy to address, and the Mac II, with 512K of memory, was already on the market. But the larger issue was that Macintosh was still very much an idiosyncratic and idealistic design in search of a real-world application—that thing that no other computer could do, that thing that made it truly indispensable, just as spreadsheets and word processing had done before it. As it happens, Jobs's departure coincided with a trio of other developments in the computer industry. Together, they would save Macintosh from the trashcan, save Apple from bankruptcy, and help inaugurate a new era for the printed word.

To be sure, the phrase "desktop publishing" did little to evoke the kind of transformative future hyped by Ridley Scott.[35] But in fact there was nothing that could be more faithful to the Mac's pedigree in Jobs's

Reed College education with Robert Palladino.[36] Besides Macintosh itself, the key technological developments were these: Apple's Laser-Writer, a laser printer the company had been developing to compete with Hewlett-Packard's LaserJet; PostScript, a language for translating the shapes of letters and images into mathematical points a laser printer could plot and draw (under development by a then-unknown company called Adobe Systems, whose founders had split from Xerox PARC; they would soon license PostScript to Apple exclusively); and a new software package called PageMaker—not Apple's either, but the product of a small start-up named, improbably, for a Renaissance-era printer and bookmaker.

With Aldus PageMaker as the layout tool, the LaserWriter as output device, and PostScript tying it all together, the Macintosh had found its killer app. If you were an individual, you could print and publish your own newsletter—people took to this idea much as they would to blogs a generation later. If you were a small business, you could produce your own catalog or calendar or brochure. Much of the ephemera and miscellany called job printing by professionals could now be created in-house.[37] And if you were an artist, a designer, or a publisher you could do your layouts in PageMaker, dump the proofs to a LaserWriter, and then, thanks to PostScript, send the exact same digital files to a professional typesetter for camera-ready copy to be printed onto films for the big industrial offset presses. Desktop publishing (the term is attributed to Aldus's founder, Paul Brainerd) became the proverbial Next Big Thing. John Warnock, Adobe's co-founder and the chief architect of PostScript, reportedly purchased a leaf from a Gutenberg Bible to display on the wall of his Mountain View office.

It was not an anomalous gesture. Computer magazines and marketing materials were suddenly rife with references to the printing press, movable type, and the "first" information revolution, what Elizabeth L. Eisenstein had only just recently characterized as a communications and cultural revolution.[38] The allusions went further: users of Aldus PageMaker were treated to a digitized rendition of Antonio Baratti's famous engraving of Manutius in profile every time they opened the software. Here too the gesture was not altogether unwarranted: Manutius was famous for printing his books—his Aldines—in small octavo formats that could be "held in the hand and learned by heart (not to speak of being read) by everyone," as he wrote.[39] The implication was obvious: anyone could be a publisher—choosing their own layouts, printing their own edition, even designing their own fonts, much as Manutius had had his cut into metal punches. The breakthrough was in the way that words and images, which had followed separate technological paths since movable type printing diverged from engraving and etching, could once again coexist within the same design and production environment throughout the publishing workflow. As one observer put it, "The power to publish resided right there on each desktop. The person at the keyboard maintained full control over content right up until the moment that the fuser unit in the laser printer solidified the electrically charged grains of toner onto the paper according to the pattern guided by the computer."[40]

Sales of Macintosh soared under the desktop publishing campaigns advanced by marketing director John Scull (not to be confused with CEO John Sculley), and Apple's fortunes were salvaged. By 1988, desktop publishing was a billion-dollar-a-year industry.[41] Adobe, of course, would go on to thrive, first introducing Illustrator (the next step up from MacPaint) then later Photoshop and of course PDF; PostScript would become an industry standard; and eventually Adobe would acquire Aldus and refactor PageMaker's code to produce the page layout program that most publishers use today, Adobe InDesign.

Little of this would presumably have been on Edward Kamau Brathwaite's mind in August 1988. Indeed, we know he would have had quite a bit much else on his mind. His first wife, Doris Monica Brathwaite, had died of cancer two years earlier, a tragedy that inaugurated a period of personal trials Brathwaite would come to call his Time of Salt. He was suffering from writer's block as a result; and with a bibliography of published work that already ran to nearly ninety pages, it was not a problem to which he would have been accustomed.[42] Brathwaite's international reputation as a poet had been secured by his first three books: *Rights of Passage* (1967), *Masks* (1968), and *Islands* (1969), all published by Oxford University Press and collected as *The Arrivants: A New World Trilogy* in 1973. He had lived and worked in the UK and Ghana (where he received the name Kamau) as well as his native Caribbean, building networks in each locale as a writer, a scholar (he earned a doctorate from the University of Sussex), a bibliographer (documenting the work of other local writers), and a publisher, running his own Savacou imprint out of Kingston, Jamaica, with the assistance of Doris Monica.

In the summer of 1988 he was at Harvard on a visiting fellowship. Like William H. Dickey, Brathwaite was no stranger to computers. Both he and Doris Monica had quickly grasped the power of word processing for their work as publishers and academics, she with a Kaypro and he learning his way around an early IBM clone called an Eagle. The Eagle computer was in fact the centerpiece of the title poem in his collection *X/Self* (1987), "X/Self's Xth Letters from the Thirteen Provinces":

> chipp/in dis poem onta dis tablet
> chiss/ellin darkness writin in light[43]

The lines are presented in Brathwaite's characteristic "nation language," his Creole or "dub" appropriation of English, replete with rhymes, puns, cacography, truncations, and eruptions of punctuation—in short, the language of Caliban. In addition to the striking conceit of writing in light (which he would return to again and again), there is the seemingly counterintuitive comparison between word processing and writing on a stone tablet, licensed here by a play on the word "chip." The "darkness," meanwhile, is not just the figurative opposite of light but also a literal rendition of the black background of the monochrome monitor the Eagle would have been outfitted with. That these were the offspring of the very same Western forces he opposed throughout his poetry was not lost on him: Brathwaite likened his computer to the Star Wars robot R2D2, to Jackie Robinson, and above all to Prospero, the Shakespearean archetype of colonial power. But Brathwaite seemed to believe that his own voice, clad first in nation language and then later in the Sycorax Video Style, inured the poetry from these contagions and might even allow his computer to dismantle the operating systems of oppressors. As he writes in "X/Self's Letters":

> for not one a we should responsible if prospero get curse
> wid him own
>
> cursor[44]

Once again Brathwaite folds the computer's idiolect into his own. Cursor is a word that does double phonetic duty, glancing as it does off both *The Tempest* and the name for the on-screen marker holding space for the user's input.

The Eagle was an ungainly and earthbound machine, not suitable for travel away from Brathwaite's home in Jamaica. So, that summer at Harvard, perhaps thinking it might spur his creativity, Brathwaite arranged for the loan of a Macintosh from a student helpdesk "that supplied tvs, radios, computers, & sundry electrical and other applian/ces etc from their office in Harvard Yaad."[45] (Meanwhile, William Dickey had just begun his HyperCard experiments a month before.) We don't know what model of Macintosh it was, but Brathwaite recounts problems with the document he was working on repeatedly crashing as he neared the end—a symptom that sounds a lot like the original Mac's notorious memory limit.[46] Nonetheless, the experience of using it seems to have been catalytic or cathartic in the way he had hoped: Brathwaite writes of developing "a very close relationship w Apple/Mac" and the following year purchasing his own "Sycorax," which is the name he gave it based on the witch who is the mother of Shakespeare's Caliban.[47] The Macintosh that Brathwaite would purchase for himself in 1989 was a Mac SE/30, so named for its 68030 processor, a slight upgrade from the original SE model Dickey was using. Brathwaite also purchased an Apple Style-Writer printer. Unlike the LaserWriter, which cost more than double the computer itself, the StyleWriter was an inkjet device, inexpensive and easily portable. It would prove central to Brathwaite's digital poetics: the "voice of the Stylewriter," he would call it, referring to "the blues of these ragged font edges."[48]

Brathwaite named his new poetics the Sycorax Video Style, or SVS for short. It refers to the manner in which he utilized the Mac's fonts and layout capabilities to orchestrate and arrange the language of his poetry on the page. Almost everything Brathwaite has published since 1990 shares a common visual aesthetic, characterized by an array of typefaces in different sizes as well as symbols, glyphs, and clip art. Often too, these are jagged or pixelated in the manner characteristic of low resolution computer displays—the "ragged edges" of which he speaks.[49] "The fonts," Brathwaite reflected, "take me across Mexico to Siqueiros and the Aztec murals and all the way back to ancient Nilotic Egypt to hieroglyphics—

the tief of his face a deceptive assassin of light
tho as i say you cdnt see that & indeed you cdnt see nothin
but this rockin & smilin triangle of the head rollin swifffly
pass the

Coast Guard Gutter

& like tic/tockin tic/tockin from side to side from the top
of the clock of his hair
& we all look at each other because we had heard that

madame

MARGARET
EUGENIA
AZUCHAR
MARKETPLACE

had at last gone up w/her harsp gruff whip & chauffeur of
a voice to !! or perhaps it was Penlyne to see what was goin
on & to give some kind of support &

macoute

to the farmers in response i suppose to my tele/phone call years
before to her on that bleach of shells where she had been able to
pick up a large pink

lambi

or conch in she horn w/out bein cut by the sharp heard cuttin edge
of the

as had happen to me when i was a likkle bwoy on a Bank Holi-
day when i was too young really to remember anything else
xcept the dunes & the bright light on all that sand of the no
hair of my youth & dazzle & the red blood from my finger
oomin down into all the coral beaches i wd ever stand on sin
ce & lookin at birds & fishes far out on the horizon

6 | A representative example of Kamau Brathwaite's Sycorax
Video Style from *DS (2): dreamstories* (2007). "Dream Haiti"
by Kamau Brathwaite, from *DS (2)*, copyright ©1989, 1994,
1995, 2000, 2002, 2007 by Kamau Brathwaite. Reprinted by
permission of New Directions Publishing Corp.

allowing me to write in light and to make sound visible as if I'm in a
video."[50]

Brathwaite's own descriptions of Sycorax, repeatedly referring to it
as a "trademark" style that he is "developing," suggest we should be able
to talk about it with some degree of material and technical specificity.
When I first delved into the scholarly literature on Brathwaite as part of
the research for my book on the literary history of word processing, I
found a robust critical conversation about the SVS illuminating the relationship between it and other aspects of postcolonial poetics as well as
its connections to Afro-Caribbean tradition and even one or two pieces
that discussed the poetry specifically in terms of digital hypertext.[51]
What was missing, however, was any extended account of the particulars of Brathwaite's actual practice and process. In so far as I could discover, we have no record of what software Brathwaite actually used

beyond the computer and printer themselves—not his preferred word processing product, nor any desktop publishing or font design program he may have had at his disposal. Nor can we identify which, if any, type-faces Brathwaite may have designed himself, despite repeated claims in the secondary literature that he has done so and despite the repeated invocation of epithets like "signature" and "trademark" to describe Sycorax itself.

One of Brathwaite's most recognizable typefaces is employed on the cover of *MiddlePassages* (1993), his first book with the important independent press New Directions.[52] Consisting of abstract, angular letterforms of minimalist stencil-like appearance—the upper-case **▲** is really just a triangular glyph with a notch on one side near the apex—it scans as futuristic and somehow non-Western. Other letters are equally unconventional: the stem of the **?** cuts out at the loop, leaving a character that resembles a question mark without a dot. The shapes have a marked pictographic quality, evoking the hieroglyphics that so compelled Brathwaite.

The typeface is called **STOP**. It had been created by an Italian typographer named Aldo Novarese in 1971.[53] Novarese, who spent his career at the Nebiolo foundry in Turin, is perhaps best known for Eurostile, readily recognized by an upper-case O with squared-off corners—like the windows of a train car it was often said, or the blocky outlines then common in architecture. ("This is the shape of our time," Novarese would write. "We see it everywhere.")[54] **STOP** represents an even further evolution of the Eurostile aesthetic, and indeed it is one of the very last typefaces Novarese was to design in his prolific career. Polarizing upon release, it was the culmination of a lifelong interest in creating for a new era of media, where large quantities of information had to be consumed and processed at great speed. The thinking among Novarese and his colleagues—heirs to Italian Futurism—was that the more abstract their letterforms became, the more easily eye and mind could scan and process them.[55] This radical reductionism was tempered by a strict internal consistency in the structural makeup of the glyphs: three vertical layers stacked with slices or spaces between. However, this desire for efficiency in fact lead to the loss of legibility: "The letters become almost abstract shapes: they no longer look like letters," in the words of one critic.[56]

STOP first appears in Brathwaite's work right around the time of *MiddlePassages'* publication.[57] There, in addition to the cover, it is also used on the interior title page and for the full-page title of two individual poems, "**WORD MAKING MAN**" and "**STONE**." An instance of it can be found in his testimonial to Doris Monica Brathwaite, *The Zea Mexican Diary 7 Sept 1926–7 Sept 1986*, published the same year by the University of Wisconsin Press. It is once again employed for an interior title page in Longman's *DreamStories* (1994); and it appears in two of the large-format books he did thereafter, *Barabajan Poems 1492–1992* (Savacou North, 1994) and *conVERSations with Nathaniel Mackey* (We Press, 1999). It was often employed for important names: **ELUEGGBA** (a Yoruban deity) in *Zea*, and Brathwaite's own name, **KAMAU**, in *Barabajan Poems*. In *Born to Slow Horses* (2005), **STOP** is used for the dedication (to "**DREAM CHAD**"). In *conVERSations* it is (uncharacteristically) employed for a longer passage on Caribbean history.

But was **STOP** Sycorax? Are the two coterminous or interchangeable with one another, semantically or otherwise? In the Brathwaite lexicon, Sycorax seemingly can refer variously to the character (Caliban's mother, the witch, in *The Tempest*), his Macintosh SE/30 as an object, a mythopoeic entity personified by the Macintosh, a distinctive aesthetic or "style," and apparently sometimes even to an individual letter, especially X, whose chiasmatic crossings reoccur throughout his poems and books. **STOP** is perhaps best thought of not as *the* actual font that is Sycorax but rather as *one* of the fonts capable of taking on the identity of Sycorax in particular settings.

From this we can appreciate what was at stake for Brathwaite in the compromises he often found himself having to make with publishers, who were confronted with the challenge of (literally) re-presenting the manuscript pages that came curling out of the StyleWriter for the typesetting processes that commercial publishing demanded. For *MiddlePassages*, New Directions adopted a hybrid approach so as to, as editor Barbara Epler put it, navigate between Brathwaite's "vision" and "reasonable traditions of design quality for New Directions."[58] Photography of Brathwaite's original pages was used to create discrete pieces of "art" (called stats) for the headline or display elements to paste into the typeset body of the text.[59] These pasted-up pages would then be photographed for films for offset printing. It was a painstaking process, and the difficultly is that it relied upon arbitrary distinctions between what elements in the poetry were appropriate for typesetting by the publisher and what needed to be cut and pasted as a stat.[60] Brathwaite, doubtless encouraged by the seamless experience of composing on the Macintosh, would have regarded his text as a unified whole. Its fragmentation into separate reproductive workflows would invariably compromise the original integrity of the work, in subtle and not-so-subtle ways.

For the cover and title page, meanwhile, New Directions insisted on adding an additional horizontal crossbar at the top of the **ꙅ** in response to concerns about its legibility.[61] (This was not inconsistent with the way **ꙅꚎOꝒ** was often employed; since its initial release, it has been widely customized and adapted as the geometric primitives of its letterforms encourage.)[62] But even that was a better outcome than Brathwaite was sometimes used to. Several years ago, I was teaching *MiddlePassages* in an undergraduate class on postmodern writing. Anticipating a lively discussion, I had begun delving into the intricacies of the Sycorax Video Style. A student interrupted, confused; she clearly had no idea what I was talking about. It turns out she had purchased the UK edition of *Middle-Passages* from the British publisher Bloodaxe Books, which had been brought out a year sooner; it included almost none of the typographic features I was enthusiastically expounding on. (A prefatory note reads "Text based on the 'Sycorax video style' being developed by Kamau Brathwaite," but the typography had been mostly flattened to a standard bookface font and one heavyweight stencil—with the conspicuous exception of "Middle Passages" on the title page, rendered in **ꙅꚎOꝒ**.)[63] This is what John Bryant asks us to call a fluid text moment: the typographic differences in the two editions—responsible for my student's confusion as well as my own initial confusion about her confusion—were products of the difficulties that inevitably arose when transposing the Sycorax style from Brathwaite's own computer and printer to the technologies and workflows of his publishers.[64]

New Directions brought out more of Brathwaite's books after *MiddlePassages*, but it would be a mistake to assume their relationship was always an easy one.[65] For *Ancestors* (2001), perhaps Brathwaite's most ambitious book, New Directions initially had one of its house designers attempt to mimic the Sycorax Video Style using the designer's own computer; despite what was obviously a protracted and painstaking process,

Kamau Brathwaite

MiDDLE
PASSAGES

BLOODAXE BOOKS

KAMAU BRATHWAITE

MiDDLE
PASSAGES

A NEW DIRECTIONS BOOK

7 & 8 | Title pages from the Bloodaxe Books and New Directions editions of Brathwaite's *MiddlePassages* (1992, 1993); note addition of the crossbar to the top of the S's in the New Directions edition, an alteration to the typeface also present on the New Directions cover (but not in any other of its interior pages). Kamau Brathwaite, *MiddlePassages* (Newcastle upon Tyne: Bloodaxe Books, 1992). Reprinted by permission of Bloodaxe Books. "Title Page" by Kamau Brathwaite, from *MIDDLEPASSAGES*, copyright ©1993 by Kamau Brathwaite. Reprinted by permission of New Directions Publishing Corp.

"Kamau dismissed it as not being at all Sycorax, unable to breathe properly, and more," a source with firsthand knowledge tells me.[66] The text was eventually photographed for film directly from Brathwaite's own manuscript, the same method New Directions would use for *DS* [*Dream Stories*] *(2)* (2007) and also adopted by several of his other publishers.[67] Even then there were trade-offs though: for example, New Directions' books were smaller than Brathwaite liked, owing to the dictates of standardized sizes for shelving; Brathwaite's self-published *Barabajan Poems* and *Ark*, as well as *conVERsations with Nathaniel Mackey*, printed by

Christopher Funkhouser's We Press, are both 8½ x 11 inches, the same dimensions as the paper sheets he fed into his printer.

Devotees of electronic literature, digital poetry, and hypertext writing often deride traditional publishing. The PUI, or Paper User Interface, was Ted Nelson's (Nelson first coined the word hypertext) pseudo-scatological term for the way computer scientists clung to anachronisms like "documents" and "pages" instead of embracing links and nodes.[68] WYSIWYG—What You See Is What You Get, the grail for word processors like MacWrite and Microsoft Word—was dismissed by Nelson and his acolytes as a failure of imagination, the computer in this view being capable of nothing Gutenberg hadn't already done some four hundred years ago. The promise of a new, infinitely more expansive Gutenberg galaxy also underwrote much of William Dickey's enthusiasm for the technology, as we have seen. But a digital poetics founded on such precepts is also arguably a poetics of Prospero. It ignores the lived realities of Brathwaite's home islands, nodes where hypertext links are impossible without the undersea cable infrastructures laid and controlled by Western telecom companies. Paper, by contrast, could partake of more localized kinds of networks: pressed metal staples instead of hardcoded links, Xerox and mimeo instead of web servers. Indeed, as Jacob Edmond has shown, Brathwaite's interest in computing and desktop publishing was consistent with a lifelong appreciation of new electronic media, including also sound recording (a number of his early poems originated as spoken-word pieces) and the Xerox machine—actual facts as Woolf might say, which made new kinds of archiving and transmission possible.[69] For Brathwaite, the power of the computer was precisely in the degree of control it promised him and the degree to which it made the production and distribution of printed matter more expedient. Brathwaite's StyleWriter was not an accessory or an afterthought to his Macintosh but the necessary terminus of a system, a final punctuation mark rendered in finely calibrated jets of ink after the restless, impermanent process of writing with light.

It is easy to be effusive, especially given the longevity and extent of Brathwaite's output with Sycorax. "The Apple Mac enabled Kamau to hold the very tool which shapes the image, to shape it himself in its minute particularities, to emphasize and sing the shapes as he creates them," enthused one contemporary observer.[70] But, as we have seen, the combination of the Macintosh SE/30 and the StyleWriter afforded Brathwaite complete creative control over his work only in so far as he did not seek to see it issued from another publisher, whose requirements and limitations would invariably introduce compromises and constraints. There were also other causes for worry. By 2004 (the same year Apple phased out HyperCard), Brathwaite describes the more-than-a-decade-old Macintosh and StyleWriter as "xhausted" and "long since out of production," a moment wherein Westernized production cycles of planned obsolescence are dramatically in tension with the slow time or slow blues of his poetics.[71] And indeed, the Mac or the printer or both reportedly soon died, probably no later than 2006.[72]

Most immediately and traumatically, this left Brathwaite without the means to compose in the Sycorax style. But it also deprived him of something even more elemental: his memory, or what Ignacio Infante characterizes as "a new archival medium."[73] Or perhaps a form of *re-memory*, in the manner we have already discussed: Brathwaite continually rewrote and republished—re-*mediated*—his work throughout his career, and the Macintosh facilitated that at a very practical level, allowing him to effortlessly retrieve the texts that it stored, and then rewrite, reformat, and otherwise rework them—a process Infante describes as a "virtual temporality in which any point in time can be retraced and accessed instantaneously."[74] Here too we can appreciate a specific technological feature of the SE/30: its internal hard drive. The hard drive, invisible and seemingly infinitely capacious, undoubtedly contributed to Brathwaite's ability to endow the computer with an autonomous agency consolidated in its identity as Sycorax. Absent diskettes to physically handle, his words were simply "in" the computer, lending further credence to its personification.

The pages of Brathwaite's printed books are a snapshot of the bitstreams that live, or once lived, on the hard drive of his Macintosh.[75] Paradoxically, however, the computer also represented the restoration of an oral tradition to Brathwaite. "The typewriter is an extension of the pen," he wrote. "The computer is getting as close as you can to the spoken word."[76] In this he was very much in sympathy with William Dickey, who as we have seen compared HyperCard first to film and animation, and then to spoken and musical performance. And yet, Dickey and Brathwaite came to negotiate the materiality of computing very differently from one other. For Dickey, the performativity of his digital compositions meant preserving that fluidity of experience by distributing the poems in their native digital format, something that, as we know, has had dire consequences for their circulation and reception. For Brathwaite, by contrast, even words written with light ultimately had to find fixity on the printed page. Working outside of the establishment channels in a postcolonial setting for much of his career, the power to publish was integral to how he thought about computers. "The computer," he wrote, echoing the widespread enthusiasm around desktop publishing, "has made it much easier for the illiterate, the Caliban, actually to get himself visible. . . . Because the computer does it all for you."[77] And yet, as Brathwaite also knew, that power was elusive, subject to the vicissitudes of commercial practices and technical or financial limitations that too often were incompatible with his vision.

Does Dickey's embrace of HyperCard suggest a certain kind of privilege—not just of access to technology and expertise, but of positioning in the canon and culture industry—that a poet like Brathwaite, working in a liminal postcolonial tradition, believed unavailable to him? Was Brathwaite simply unwilling to risk any distribution channel for his poetry lacking the cultural authority of print? It would seem so. But one can also see in Brathwaite's continual republishing and remediation of his printed books a way of capturing something of the fluid and aleatory nature of composition on the screen, something that both he and Dickey apprehended so powerfully. Chris Funkhouser, who worked closely with Brathwaite to publish *conVERSations*, compared him to a DJ, noting that he "takes one text and makes/records/creates incredible restructuring of it, an expansion, then goes back and makes 'perfect' adjustments in 'mixing' final edits."[78]

We can observe this practice in the increasingly detailed colophons Brathwaite began attaching to his work through the 1990s and early 2000s, specifying dates and times for revision (very much like the metadata in digital files) as well as word counts, place, accidents of composition, and sometimes incidentals of mood: "rev again 21 Nov 03 & 21 Oct 05/5:10am-9:45am and all afternoon of Oct 27 05 to the usual 3:am in the miggle," reads one, printed in a book called *DS (2)*. "reform for NewDirections 23-24-25 July 03 (all-night to 5:35 am & there's quiet sunlight outside!)" reads another.[79]

But even this was to prove too terribly fragile and illusory: "because of loss of Sycorax memory. certain dying fonts. like Salt Eliot's poems they are. they will not stay will not stay in place will not stay still now."[80]

In *DreamStories* (1998), Kamau Brathwaite recounts a disquieting episode in which messages suddenly began appearing unbidden on the screen of his borrowed Macintosh, as though the machine had a spirit or intelligence of its own—or as if someone else was using it.[81] In fact, the SE was equipped to handle the new AppleTalk protocol, through which such messages could conceivably have been sent. Regardless, let us say the following message now appears—unbidden—on the page before us at the conclusion of this chapter:

```
A recent Digital Humanities lecture presented
both a fount and a font of information about a
poem's unusual digital typeface but not a word
about the font's meaning or ideology or how the
visual display affected the interpretation of the
poem. This was New Criticism with close reading
not of the words of a text but the technology
for generating its letters.[82]
```

In fact, the originator of this message is a poet and critic I admire and whose work I have always found inspiring. More to the point, he had been in the audience at Penn. I would stumble across the comment on his Facebook page not long after. It stung, of course. I quickly typed and just as quickly purged several different responses: "Digital humanities? Who said anything about digital humanities? This is bibliography, bub!" or else "Yes! Exactly right. It was a close reading of a technology. STOP originated not in Brathwaite's native Caribbean or in Nilotic Egypt, but in a type foundry in Northern Italy; its distinctive geometry enfolds a unique geography, as well as a set of localized industrial and artisanal pressures which (quite literally) shaped it." Or else again: "Meaning? Ideology? Must everything always be sanctioned by interpretation and critique?" (This last in particular seemed an odd defense to need to muster for the sake of one whose career has been so artfully devoted to glancing off the edges of meanings.) I felt I would have been justified in invoking surface reading or "the limits of critique" or media archaeology and what Wolfgang Ernst calls archaeography, which is the machine archive writing itself with its own instruments on its own terms.

There is also of course ample precedent for bibliography distancing itself from anything so mundane as literary meaning. There is W. W. Greg's oft-quoted pronouncement: "Bibliography is the study of books as tangible objects. It examines the materials of which they are made and the manner in which those materials are put together. It traces their place and mode of origin, and the subsequent adventures that have befallen them. It is not concerned with their contents in a literary sense."[83] There is Randall McLeod's longstanding habit of examining books upside down so as not to succumb to the temptation of actually reading them. Ultimately Greg's and McLeod's precepts are both compatible with Claude Shannon's exclusion of meaning from the foundational concerns of signal transmission.[84] But whereas Shannon neglects the blank box that is his unlabeled stand-in for the ineluctable materiality of that process ("mere medium"), bibliographers focus on little else.

Part of me was—still is—unwilling to concede that this is not enough. "I am here to contribute to certain facts of the matter. It is an honest day's work," I could imagine saying, adding: "Let someone else take what I have done and produce a 'reading' if they feel they must." But the real problem is not that someone else might produce a reading more compelling than any I myself can offer, but that someone else might strain mightily to do so and find that they are unable. What if, in the end, the facts of the matter (or at least, *these* facts, as they pertain to ꗉ) don't make any difference at all? What if such details exceed not only the hermeneutical horizon, but indeed any and all conceivable epistemological horizons, as would, presumably, say, the question of what color socks Brathwaite was wearing on the day he composed a certain poem? (Or was he barefoot?)

Again, we might take recourse in the pronouncement of Ezra Pound by way of Lawrence Rainey: if the more we know of Eliot the better, then so too the more we know of Brathwaite. Bibliography as a habit of mind might permit me to stop there. But there are additional considerations we can muster. First, the clear codependence of the Sycorax Video Style and Brathwaite's poetics suggests the desirability of understanding what Sycorax actually was and wasn't, not just aesthetically or mythopoeically, but also, yes, typographically and technologically. Second, Brathwaite himself placed such a premium on the physical presentation of his books that it seems an odd and untenable asymmetry to have particulars pertaining to their material makeup be forever unknown. I think, for example, of Joseph Viscomi's work on William Blake's relief-etching methods. He furnished the first full and accurate account of the process of illuminated printing by calling upon his own training as a printmaker to recreate Blake's methods, using only such tools and materials as would have been available to Blake in the eighteenth century.[85] Viscomi's findings, in turn, have been brought back into critical readings of Blake, in effect restoring Blake the printer to the dyad of the Blake the poet and the painter.

How would it change our reading of a poem if we had access to the complete "menu" of fonts on the computer from which Brathwaite had to choose and if we then knew that he selected this one and not that one out of a finite set that we could survey? Likewise, questions about whether Brathwaite created his own fonts versus amassing them from various Western sources would seem to have implications for any postcolonial reading of his work. One can imagine the argument about Brathwaite rejecting the tools of Prospero in order to fashion his own; one could equally well imagine an argument about his rewriting and refashioning of them. But the fact is there were many hundreds if not thousands of third-party Macintosh fonts then in circulation, and whether Brathwaite did or did not design his own is not something we can determine absent his own comment on the matter (I have found none), a forensic examination of his Macintosh SE/30 (its present whereabouts are unknown), or a systematic appraisal by an expert typographer (not something I am equipped to produce or sponsor).[86]

Bibliographers are accustomed to uncertainty. In an eloquent essay on the humble composing stick, Joseph A. Dane remarks almost offhandedly, "We simply do not know how type was set in the fifteenth and sixteenth centuries."[87] What he is really saying is that we don't know nearly as much as we would like to know about the process, and the people who would know—because they were there, doing it—are long gone. Perhaps unexpected, though, is uncertainty in such close proximity to the present. Brathwaite, while he was living, was not responsive to my several contacts. (I do not begrudge him!) I did speak with several close associates, but none could answer questions about his fonts and software with the exactness I sought—indeed, more than one told me it would never have occurred to them to ask about such things in the first place. What seems to be at issue here is the degree to which we are still unaccustomed to thinking about the bitstream at the level of specificity bibliography demands of us. We reflexively relegate such details to the realm of inconsequential minutiae, which becomes a black box (or a sock drawer) of our own making.

But it is still worth questioning the origins and motivations—indeed, the basic epistemological assumptions—that drive our yearning for such knowledge. In a provocative essay, scholar of indigenous textuality Matt Cohen argues that even the newfound interest in what he terms "digital bibliographical mediation" may be a colonizing gesture, assuming as it does that implicit contrasts between old and new are universals.[88] Both the coming and going of Dickey's HyperPoems and their attendant hardware, and the persistent precarity of Brathwaite's Macintosh and printer would seem to confirm the utility of that stance. Moreover, bibliography cannot assume a universal archive. The kind of detail whose deficiency I bemoan with regard to Brathwaite's computing environment is merely a recent and comparatively benign manifestation of a long chain of archival silences and violences, as Toni Morrison clearly knew when writing of rememory. Powerfully, Cohen points to one of Morrison's predecessors, the African American novelist Pauline Elizabeth Hopkins, whose literary assets are omitted from her probate records, which list only her wardrobe and more mundane possessions.[89] This is, as Cohen recognizes, the kind of exclusion that animates a scholar such as Saidiya Hartman and her methodology of critical fabulation: a form of reparative storytelling, based not on archival or material evidence but a different kind of imperative. "This may mean," as Cohen puts it, "doing bibliography with different chronicities and evidentiary standards in mind; with different communities' protocols and well-being as guides; with different collaborators than customary; and with a more explicit political awareness than has often attended bibliographical work."[90]

To the best of my knowledge, no prior commentator on Brathwaite has identified ꙅꚍOP—one of the most distinctive fonts in his oeuvre—by name. Doing so does not, it is true, immediately yield up a decisive new interpretation of the poems in *MiddlePassages* or elsewhere. But imagine this. Imagine Brathwaite's hand on his mouse. Imagine the mouse's pointer on the monochrome screen of his Mac SE/30. Now imagine him pulling down a menu of font choices, alphabetized and each displayed in its own unique face. He scrolls through them, first down, then up, then down again. As he scrolls, the title of the book on the screen, whose letters Brathwaite has highlighted, ripples in an accompanying typographic medley. Then he pauses and decides, and the letters on the screen go still, instantly assuming their new shapes. Given that the title of his book of poems refers to the barbarous and often lethal transport of Africans to enslavement in the Caribbean and Americas (to say nothing of other, ongoing injustices as evidence by the title's plural), it is possible perhaps to read in the name of the typeface Brathwaite so deliberately selected a simple and uncompromising injunction:

STOP

3 | The Story of S.

Somewhere amid the wailing of *The Gutenberg Elegies*—his jeremiad against "the Faustian pact" between literature and digital media, first published in 1994—critic and essayist Sven Birkerts offers up an anecdote from his days as a bookseller. He has arrived at the home of a still youthful English professor, who shows him into an immaculate and exclusive library of nineteenth- and twentieth-century literature, hundreds and hundreds of carefully curated volumes. He wants to sell every last one. Inquiries are made: Are you sick? Moving? "No. But I'm getting out of books." He then brings Birkerts down to the basement, where there is a computer, screen aglow amid the gloom. "I'm changing my life," he tells an astonished Birkerts. "This is definitely where it's all going to happen."[1]

There are a couple of things about this set piece that don't quite pass the sniff test, not least that exactly how the precocious professor plans to change his life (and still put food on the table) remains unspoken. Then there is the obligatory descent to the underworld, where engines of darkness await. Nonetheless, I called the episode to mind one afternoon a couple of years ago whenI found myself going down a flight of basement steps in a row house in Washington, D.C. I was visiting a concern called Asia Pacific Offset—not a publisher or a printer, but a "print management" firm. I wasn't sure quite what I expected to find there: an office I supposed, which indeed is what it was. And, of course, there were computers, outfitted with wide-screen plasma displays already a generation beyond the Dell I had seen at Princeton (they would have sent Birkerts's 1994 persona reeling into a catatonia). But there were also shelves and shelves of books in that basement room. And these books—all of them—*looked* fabulous. I mean just that. They were not old books. They were breathtakingly, uninhibitedly *new*, a riot of colors and textures and trim sizes, with luxurious art and typography and stitching; gift books and novelty books, art books and coffee table books, specialty and custom books. Books, I often say to my students, look really, really good these days: have you noticed? (They smell really good too: not dust and old leather but the sweetness of ink and industrial sealants.)

One of the books I see on the shelves is eponymously entitled *The Book*. It's easy to spot because it sports fire engine red binding tape and large white sans-serif capitals on the spine. Subtitled *A Cover-to-Cover Exploration of the Most Powerful Object of Our Time*, *The Book* is a book about books by Keith Houston published by W. W. Norton in 2016. It is a well-written and generously illustrated non-specialist's introduction to the history of the book and bibliography, appearing in the market more than two decades into the digital dark age Birkerts was so desperate to ward or wish away. *The Book* is a bravura production: as an object it presents itself as an embodied but exploded instance of its subject, with material features like headcap, spine, endpapers, ornaments, running heads and more, all explicitly marked and labeled. This is effective for the neophyte but it also subtlety reinforces the anxieties around identity that seem constantly to beset this, the most powerful object of our time. The very first sentence of *The Book* declares "this is a book," before adding "until recently, a book was a book and the word came without caveats."[2] *The Book* aspires to be a proxy for *the* book in its most idealized form, or what Houston terms "the *bookness* of . . . books," themselves "unrepentantly analog contraptions of paper, ink, cardboard, and glue."[3]

The Book is here in this basement I am visiting because it is a book Asia Pacific was retained for. Though Norton is its publisher, the actual book (as is typical of most books nowadays) was put together elsewhere, and by others' hands. The production was outsourced to a designer who lives in a town of 1,600 in the Catskills, and the printing was done in Guongdong Province, China. The paper was sourced from a vendor in Taiwan.[4] It is Asia Pacific's role to oversee and coordinate all these relationships and many others besides in the globalized supply chain required to make—or "manufacture," as the copyright page explicitly has it—*The Book* as a saleable product. Asia Pacific keeps offices here in D.C. as well as New York, Hong Kong, and in a half dozen other cities integral to the global book trade. As for the company name, that too is not incidental: owing to reduced labor costs, southeast China and Hong

Kong are the center of the world's printing industry for illustrated and full-color books.[5]

Far-flung offices and occasional site visits notwithstanding, the vast majority of Asia Pacific's work is done by computer and internet. The bitstream is thus an integral part of the workflow of contemporary bookmaking. Robert Darnton's famous communications circuit is now literalized as an actual circuit, or more accurately, what is termed a supply chain, each link knowing just enough about its predecessor and successor to maintain the flow, but only a few (like Asia Pacific) with access to the complete picture.[6] (Very much like the way the bitstream itself moves through the internet in discrete packets, just as Claude Shannon foresaw.) The common denominator in all this is that a book is, in practice, an assemblage of digital files that can be shunted around the globe more or less at will—a far cry from the paper, ink, cardboard, and glue that *The Book* announces as its indexical status. Not until hardware converts these digital files into thermal polymer plates for printing on (computer-controlled) offset presses does the book assume anything close to an inviolate material form. *The Book*, so unrelentingly bookish in its staged presentation, remains a book—which is to say the potential for it to become a book again and again through printing innumerable copies—by virtue of the collected digital assets that are, in truth, *The Book*.

There is nothing exceptional in any of that. Just as many manuscripts (like our poet's in the introduction) begin life as electronic documents, so too do nearly all books now begin life as virtual simulacra, their wireframe margins and scalable vector edges rasterized against a pixel-perfect grid that defines what will become the book's volumetric dimensions once fabricated as an object.[7] The most important piece of software in the contemporary book world is not Microsoft Word, nor is it a web browser or Amazon's Kindle app. The most important piece of software in the publishing world today is Adobe InDesign, part of the Adobe Creative Suite and based on the original Aldus PageMaker. "InDesign," notes one reference, "cannot be thought of as any kind of word processing program. It is more like a drawing program in which you make shapes and then pour text into the shapes."[8] If, as I tried to show in *Track Changes*, word processing's root logics were managerial, then InDesign's descend from the traditions of commercial art direction. Whereas one typically views a Word document in vertically scrolled

9 | *Bitstreams* as a bitstream (which is to say, a digital file), rendered in Adobe InDesign, the software environment in which this book was typeset and designed. Screenshot courtesy of the University of Pennsylvania Press.

pages, for example, InDesign's default view is two facing pages called a spread. Text is not copied and pasted in InDesign, it is *placed*, the command a holdover from the day when typeset sheets were manually fastened to boards to produce camera-ready copy. The root logic of InDesign is thus *control*. Its rulers and guides, its grids, its precision tools for the placement of margins and edges, its layers and libraries all speak to the desire to achieve mastery over the book as form: "pixel-perfect," in Adobe's own parlance.

Like QuarkXPress and Aldus PageMaker before it, Adobe InDesign seeks to create a framework for allowing its user to work with disparate media types within a common environment while generating the digital assets necessary to advance a "book" through the different stages of a publishing workflow. Functionally, InDesign allows the user to collocate media assets of many different formats within unified data structures like "stories." It also assumes responsibility for coordinating all these different assets in such a way as to ensure their integrity as a single coherent data package that can be managed and migrated as appropriate through the production cycle. Here is how one Jack Noel, age twenty-eight, working as a book designer for Walker Books (which occupies several floors of an old mattress factory in Vauxhall), describes his lot:

> Every day is kind of the same—sit at a Mac, flick between En-
> tourage, Photoshop, InDesign and Firefox, drink coffee in the
> morning, tea in the afternoon, eat custard creams throughout. And
> every day is different—the process of designing a cover takes ages
> and at any one time I'll be working on at least half a dozen titles. I
> might be working on, say, a vampire love story, a romance anthol-
> ogy, historic fiction, an urban thriller and a graphic novel—in fact
> that's pretty much exactly what I've got on right now.[9]

This description of contemporary bookmaking (biscuit crumbs and all) is not unlike the gritty accounts of early modern printing that descend to us from figures such as Joseph Moxon in his *Mechanick Exercises* (1683).[10] But the experience of our latter-day Moxon in a South London loft with custard creams and the Adobe Creative Suite is balanced by the fact that most books published today would not exist without a global infrastructure and supply chain that consists not only of publishers and designers but also management services (like Asia Pacific), printers and binderies, packagers, suppliers, warehouses, distributors, agents, sales reps, trade fairs, and more. Unlike the example of the eighteenth-century bookseller Pierre Rigaud in Darnton's account, this circuit is far beyond the ken of most individuals. Books, in other words, are fully integrated global commodities. The bitstream is what mediates between any one person's work day and the vast network that makes up the industry.[11]

Paul Luna has made the point that typesetting in particular is now an activity that is distributed among authors, copyeditors, and design-ers: "The boundaries between the tools that printers use to typeset and make books, and the tools that authors use to write, and publishers use to edit, have dissolved," he concludes.[12] There were even earlier indica-tors. In 1995, Douglas Coupland published *Microserfs*, his fictionalized take on the khaki-clad riot nerds of the computer revolution. In it, coders low on the ladder at Microsoft make the great migration south to Silicon Valley to take a shot at being 1.0 with their own start-up. The product Daniel and his friends are designing is called *Oop!*, an Object Oriented Lego play-kit a little like *Minecraft* avant la lettre. But *Oop!* is the novel's MacGuffin. Coupland wrote *Microserfs* when the desktop publishing industry we surveyed in chapter 2 was fully mature. A graduate of design school at Emily Carr in Vancouver, he had first encountered the Macintosh—and the page design program QuarkXPress—nearly a decade earlier.[13] "In 1982 there were maybe 50,000 in North America who knew what kerning is," he once observed. "Today, my 10-year-old nephew knows what it is."[14] The characters in *Microserfs* discourse as breezily about fonts as they do EPROM memory chips and Kraft cheese slices—like the Lego sculptures studding their downtown Palo Alto office, type is simply part of the texture of the world they inhabit, never further than the nearest drop-down menu. At one point we're given a jokey list of nine different speed settings for a blender, complete with the detail that they were printed in "7-point Franklin Gothic."[15]

But *Microserfs* is most notable for Coupland's own typographic explorations. Ostensibly artifacts of the digital journal Daniel keeps on his PowerBook, these take the form of eruptions of words arranged like refrigerator poetry in oversized Helvetica. Fonts, the visible expression of the alternate consciousness inside Daniel's laptop—not so much Intel Inside as Id Inside—are the *body* of the book, an optical counterweight to its rarefied discourse on coding. Fonts and layouts, in other words, are the typographic correlates to the characters' obsession with Shiatsu massage and body building; every few pages they disrupt the regular story arc in favor of words that take on meaning through visual juxtaposition and non-linear associations. When Daniel's mother suffers a stroke and is only able to communicate by typing in 36-point letterforms on the screen of a Mac, her inert "crashed" body visibly fuses with the digital subconscious of the text—an emotional catharsis materially afforded by the everyday wonders of TrueType and PostScript.

Coupland himself referred to these typographic effects as the "look-feel" of the book, a term he consciously adopted from the software industry. His methods—and especially the manner in which he operates as both author and designer—preceded a wave of books published by figures as diverse as Mark Danielewski, Steve Tomasula, Shelley Jackson, Warren Lehrer, Anne Carson, Thalia Field, Zachary Thomas Dodson, Matthew McIntosh, and Leanne Shapton, among others.[16] Danielewski, best known for *House of Leaves* (which he flew to New York to typeset himself in the corner of his publisher Pantheon's office), maintains what he calls an "atelier" in Los Angeles, where writers, artists, designers, and media specialists gather to plan and produce the volumes of his twenty-seven-part book series (modeled on long-form TV), *The Familiar*.[17] All of this is enabled by the ease with which text and images, words and art can be blended and flowed in the Adobe environment, with print-ready PDFs transmitted to production facilities anywhere in the world. While the authors I named here specialize in particularly extravagant kinds of bookish productions over which they preside as auteurs, the underlying technology and processes are much the same for more conventional titles.

A book today—yes, even this one—is a type of bookish media. By bookish media I don't have in mind what Mindell Dubansky playfully terms "blooks" (objects that look like books but are not), nor arch meditations on "books as furniture," or the sort of performative bookwork cataloged by Garrett Stewart.[18] I would also wish to distinguish or at least differently inflect bookish media from what Jessica Pressman has influentially identified as an "aesthetics of bookishness," in which texts seek to flaunt their material status as books in order to assert (and memorialize) the codex in a time of technological transition.[19] By contrast, for me bookish media names the way in which books have been fully subsumed by the homology of contemporary media. Some books—relatively few, but in increasing numbers—arguably cannot be meaningfully read apart from a network of associated content in other formats. They function as no mere adaptations or tie-ins but as continuations or extensions of films, games, graphic novels, and other consumables. It is true that books have been nodes in transmedia networks before: witness *Uncle Tom's Cabin* and the onslaught of derivative, racist, and often grotesque texts, objects, and stage performances that were a staple of nineteenth-century popular culture. But invoking such precedents also risks a crude historicism: when data from a live-action motion capture is used to virtually animate a character in a computer-generated film—even as that same motion capture data becomes the basis for a full 360° rendering of the character in a video game—and is then used to define the proportions of a line of action figures fabricated from a digital wireframe—this presents us with a very different mode of production from that which obtained when a nineteenth-century craftsman cast a porcelain figurine of Uncle Tom based on his description in the novel, or the physique of the stage actor he might have seen playing the character the night before.

So I mean that books are a type of media, yes, but also and more specifically that books, by virtue of the bitstream, now share deep ontological commitments and compatibilities with other media types and formats, participating in the same technologies and infrastructures and economy.[20] Which is also to say it is not obvious that the making of books is materially different from that of most other commodities in a global system. Just as there is nothing unique about the ones and zeros in the bitstream of a book's digital assets, there is also nothing very distinctive about books logistically. (Jeff Bezos started Amazon with books because books were amenable to just the kind of modularization supply chains demand.) Raw materials for making books are sourced from vendors in a global marketplace. Newly printed, books go into a cargo container where they will spend weeks or months on the water. Asia Pacific oversees all of this for its clients, together with warehousing and distribution. (Its agents have been known to crawl inside shipping containers to assess their watertight integrity.)[21] The air of exceptionalism that has animated so much of the history of the book in other eras vanishes now. The book may be a mighty frigate but it rides the waves on the behemoth hulls of Maersk and MSC. And as Marc Levinson and others have taught us, a shipping container is a shipping container regardless of what it contains—as much a "box" in this way as the one at the center of Claude Shannon's diagram.[22]

The homogenization of the bitstream finds its most enduring expression in the so-called convergence narrative, a view of media production and consumption that has been articulated in remarkably similar ways in the writings of such otherwise different thinkers as Ithiel de Sola Pool, Bill Gates, and Friedrich Kittler. As Pool explains, "A process called the 'convergence of modes' is blurring the lines between media, even between point-to-point communications, such as the post, telephone, and telegraph, and mass communications, such as the press, radio, and television. A single physical means—be it wires, cables or airwaves—may carry services that in the past were provided in separate ways. Conversely, a service that was provided in the past by any one medium—be it broadcasting, the press, or telephony—can now be provided in several different physical ways."[23] Gates is more succinct: "Because all kinds of information can be stored in digital form, documents containing all kids of information will get easier and easier to find, store, and send across a network."[24] For purposes of the bitstream then, convergence narratives rest on the binary symbolic representational scheme at the heart of modern computing. Here, as we have seen, there is no ontological difference between a string of ones and zeros representing text and a string of ones and zeros representing music or a film. Kittler compares the moment to the "monopoly" of alphabetic representation over cultural memory prior to the advent of recorded sound and images. "What will end in the monopoly of bits and fiber optics began with the monopoly of writing," he declares.[25]

Yet convergence also begets divergence. Henry Jenkins, who has been one of the most important writers on the topic of media convergence, makes this point by way of what he terms the black box fallacy. "I don't know about you," Jenkins writes, "but in my living room, I am seeing more and more black boxes. There are my VCR, my digital cable box, my DVD players, my digital recorder, my sound system, and my two game systems. . . . The perpetual tangle of cords that stands between me and my 'home entertainment' center reflects the degree of incompatibility and dysfunction that exist between various media technologies."[26] This passage recalls Jonathan Sterne's vignette of drawers and shelves overflowing with the cables and cords that are the residue of prior computing regimens. Convergence, to the extent it exists, is an artful effect, sustained (more or less) by engineering, ecosystems, exploitative labor practices, and rare earth mineral mining, to say nothing of tariffs and treaties, international standards, and copyright and intellectual property enforcement. We are once again talking about materiality: the materiality of the storage, infrastructure, platforms, standards, and formats, as well as the material heterogeneity of the bitstream, a material heterogeneity imposed by the competing formal logics for the interpretation of the ubiquitous ones and zeros of bytes themselves.

What is a book nowadays? The good news for book scholars is that books are as much of a mess as they've always been. As digital workflows have overtaken publishing, we see media converging in a common application environment, we see roles and responsibilities converging within a single individual or at least a smaller subset of them than would have previously been the case, and we see output options converging within a single master file that can generate derivatives in multiple formats on demand. Books exist in a new kind of relationship to other media—by which I mean not just the homogeneity of the binary code uniting an InDesign file and an MPEG movie, but also in how they behave in the spectrum of content and services we consume. Books are messy then still, but books are also produced, circulated, and above all controlled as media properties by multinational corporations that count as their subsidiaries the Big Five of contemporary publishing, responsible for some 80 percent of books published in the United States alone.

By skewing the nominal "book" into the adjective of bookish media, I mean to suggest that what makes—*makes*—a book is a set of qualities or affordances that can be modeled and simulated by software and synthesized through fabrication processes themselves impossible to execute without the aid of sophisticated digital design and production equipment. A well-rehearsed example is Jonathan Safran Foer's latticework *Tree of Codes*, which, as both Pressman and Steven E. Jones have noted, could not exist without the benefit of CNC controllers and the software used to design not only the book but the dies from which its pages are machine-cut.[27] (In a very real sense, we can now print the press that prints the book.) Or as I've said elsewhere, the bitstream hasn't abolished books in the crude sense forecast by Birkerts; it has absorbed and remade them.[28] Books, we can say, have emerged from the other side of the digital's disruption with their material forms intact, but also irrevocably changed—"post-digital," in the rubric of media theorist Florian Cramer.[29]

Let's now turn to the story of one particular book and its making: J. J. Abrams and Doug Dorst's *S.,* first published October 29, 2013, in an edition of 145,000 copies by Mulholland Books, an imprint of Little, Brown, whose parent company in New York is Hachette, itself owned by the Lagardère Group, a multinational headquartered in Paris.

S is a book, of that there is no question. S. is also, as every commen-tator notes, a book-within-a-book. To read S. means removing its shrink-wrap, breaking a seal, and then sliding a volume bearing the title *The Ship of Theseus* from a slipcase with an embossed and emblazoned blackletter S. S. is thus a book squared—two books in one—but it also a book that doubles down on the idea of its being a book. Book squared but also the square root of book, if you will.

Sibilant soundings are an opportune starting point, duplicating as they do the serpentine logic of S. *The Ship of Theseus* is (purportedly) written by one V. M. Straka, purportedly originally in Czech and trans-lated by one F. X. Caldeira, and purportedly published in 1949 by the Winged Shoes Press of New York. It is 472 pages, 6.5 x 9.7 inches, cloth bound, sewn. A library sticker with a Dewey Decimal call number (813.54 STR 1949) adheres to the bottom quadrant of the spine, and the inside cover is stamped BOOK FOR LOAN (while the back cover has a couple of dozen variously inked and stamped checkout dates from 1957 to 2000). Along the way there have been some stormy seas, for the interior pages are weathered and stained. *Ship of Theseus* is centered on a protag-onist identified only as S., a sailor suffering from amnesia. But that is (quite literally) only part of the story, for in the margins of the book we find messages and comments "handwritten" by two additional protag-onists, Eric and Jen, who swap it back and forth with one another, using it as the bark for their own epistolary romance. *The Ship of Theseus* thus presents itself as a found object, a conceit further reinforced by the plethora of ephemera that comes tucked into its pages: postcards, no-tecards, newspaper clippings, campus stationary, business cards, pho-tographs, a code-wheel, even a paper napkin imprinted with the name of a faux coffee franchise.

In as much as this maze might amaze us, it is only half the story in another sense as well, which is to say that the circumstances of the book's production are at least as telling as the snaking strands of its metafictional premise. For S. is also very much the intertwined story of the collaboration between film and television producer J. J. Abrams and the novelist Doug Dorst, both of whose names appear on the spine of the slipcase. But that too is only a beginning. As mentioned, S. is issued under the imprint of Mulholland Books, but there are two additional logos to be seen on the packaging: Bad Robot (which is Abrams's pro-

10 | Abrams and Dorst's *S.*, or *Ship of Theseus* (2013), with slipcase and inserts. Note the "marginalia" in the book and the distressed look of the pages, all identical from one copy to another. Photo courtesy of Melcher Media.

duction company) and Melcher Media, a concern dedicated to the "art and science of storytelling."[30]

Melcher, whose name originates with founder Charles Melcher, is not a design house; nor is it a publisher. Sited in modest rooms in (another) basement, this time of a brownstone in lower Manhattan, Melcher is contracted by publishers who need a small, elite team to develop story concepts into fully realized book products. (In the business, this is known as book packaging.) Melcher's contributions may involve specs for artwork and layout as well as unique casings, bindings, paper stocks, pop-ups, inserts, and so forth—all the actual material stuff of a book, sourced from global supply chains with which Melcher maintains a far-flung web of connections. Founded in 1994, Melcher has a history of innovating around the materials science of bookmaking, including Charles Melcher's patent for DuraBook, a plastic-fiber recyclable all-weather substitute for paper. (Melcher's DuraBook titles range from *Aqua Erotica: 18 Stories for a Steamy Bath*—where the waterproofing was necessary for obviously compelling reasons—to *Cradle to Cradle*, a sustainable book by ecologist William McDonough.) Melcher has built a client list of big-brand entertainment tie-ins—the companion book for the musical *Hamilton*, for example—but it was also behind the production of Al Gore's *An Inconvenient Truth*. It delivered a blinding hot pink faux-alligator skin cover for the HBO series *Sex and the City*, and a squishy gel-filled cover for a Nickelodeon retrospective.

Melcher has carved out a particular niche for affordable mass-market books that are designed—*made*—to look like other, older books: that is, exaggerated caricatures of the codex form typically achieved through generously applied layers of artificial age and distress and self-conscious reference to the most conspicuous features of book design from previous eras, like raised bands on the spine. Melcher books in this fashion include the aforementioned *Hamilton* volume as well as a similar one for the Broadway show *Wicked* (fashioned to look like a book of spells), a tie-in for a video game (*Tom Clancy's The Division*) and at least two other TV series, *Mr. Robot* and *Stranger Things*, as well as its masterpiece, which is of course *S*. All of these projects were done in collaboration with HeadCase Design, a Philadelphia-based studio run by Paul Kepple.

My use of "layers" just above may present a confusion—do I mean layers literally, or as some sort of digital effect? This ambiguity is salutary since Melcher and HeadCase rely on precisely a symbiosis of digital embellishment and materials science—realized through access to a global supply chain, itself exquisitely mediated through digital systems—in the design and production processes. All of these books feature pages meant to appear aged or damaged.[31] Some are blackened or scorched, as if coated with soot or ash; other pages exhibit signs of foxing or mold or water damage. Page edges are often deckled as well as ragged or torn. The back cover of one title is stippled, as if sandblasted; close examination of multiples reveals that these pinprick imprints are all positioned in exactly the same spot on each copy. Sometimes this approach gets a client into trouble; Melcher books have garnered angry Amazon comments from customers who think they were sent a used or damaged book instead of the pristine one they believe they paid for.[32]

When it came time to do the tie-in for Netflix's series *Stranger Things*, Melcher and HeadCase were prepared. Released in 2018, *Stranger Things: Worlds Turned Upside Down* is presented as though it were an eighties-era Stephen King–style hardcover salvaged from a used book bin, complete with a price-gun sticker marking its condition as FAIR from Melvald's General Store. The jacket's corners and edges are tattered and uneven, though (again) examination of multiple copies betrays the uniform die-cutting behind the effect. Unfortunately, these artificial tears also rendered the jacket vulnerable to the possibility of tearing for real when the books were packaged and shipped. Similarly, the jacket is of an unlaminated stock authentic for the period, but that left it susceptible to *actual* damage and wear as copies rubbed against each other in transit. The publisher, Penguin Random House, was concerned; so, the team added a crinkly Mylar cover of the sort that is frequently found

11 | Dust jacket for *Stranger Things: Worlds Turned Upside Down*, produced by Melcher Media (2018). All of the wear and distress is artificially induced, a mixture of die-cutting and color printing (note the "Don't Freak!" sticker). Photo courtesy of Melcher Media.

sheathing library and second-hand books. This served the dual purpose of actually protecting the product *and* enhancing its period appearance. Buyers will discover that it comes with an additional peel-off sticker informing them that all these features are deliberate. ("Don't freak!" it reads. "This book is supposed to look worn and torn.")

All these productions are obvious instances of what Pressman names as the aesthetics of bookishness. Nostalgia is the principle affective register in their design and presentation, the end goal of all the Photoshop and Illustrator layers and all the materials sourced from the furthest reaches of the supply chain. But while this is the aesthetics of bookishness, it is not totemic or fetishistic as are the majority of Pressman's examples; neither is it mournful or melancholic, it seems to me. This aesthetic is, instead, *immersive*, and to that end, earnest. Melcher books are meant to be taken as what are called in-world objects, literal tangible extrusions from a collective storyworld. The *Hamilton* book is meant to look like a book Alexander Hamilton would have had on his own shelf, with ostensibly hand-tooled work on the two-toned faux-leather spine between raised bands (which, of course, are hollow skeuomorphs). *Wicked* is put forward as the grimoire that appears in the show; likewise, the marbled composition book for *Mr. Robot: Red Wheelbarrow* is based on a notebook that figures in the second season of the series. Melvald's General Store is an actual fictional locale in the town of Hawkins where *Stranger Things* is set. The effect perhaps goes furthest in *Tom Clancy's The Division: New York Collapse*, "an interactive adventure" that ties into the Clancy game, *The Division*, from Ubisoft and Red Storm Entertainment. The book is presented as an artifact extruded from the game's post-apocalyptic setting, within which players may indeed encounter it in its virtual rendition (or edition). In the classic Baudrillardian sense, the book we hold in our hands is a simulacrum, not just because every copy is identical but because aspects of it are derived from the same digital assets used to render the virtual game object. In all of these instances, books, rather than being singled out as exceptional—sites of the fetish or totem—are treated as consensual hallucinations enabled by the continuity and internal consistency of the encompassing franchise and brand. And in the case of *S.*, the book isn't just a tie-in or artifact of the storyworld, it *is* the storyworld, as literally for us the reader, who holds it in our hands, as it is for Eric and Jen, whose "hands"—we are meant to accept—once clasped these very same boards.

Reading *S.*, then, involves a very elementary suspension of disbelief: we must each of us pretend that our own individual copy is unique, a one-of-a-kind found object and precisely *not* the manufactured item whose status as a mass-produced commodity is what allows it to come into our possession in the first place. Such a suspension of disbelief is entirely consistent with details of the design and fabrication process, which have been documented through a number of journalistic accounts. One of the most detailed, published in a trade design journal called *PaperSpecs*, introduces *S.* as "the most complex project of 2013."[33] *S.* was in fact produced over an intense six-month period in the first half of 2013. Dorst had delivered a Word file with the full text of the novel by February; the book was set to go to press by July for an October release. The single most pervasive design feature to be accounted for was the marginal discourse of Eric and Jen, present on almost every page of the book. Each of them has their own distinct script, and each writes (and sometimes draws) with multiple implements and inks in different colors. *The Ship of Theseus* text constituted the main body of Dorst's electronic document file, whereas the marginalia took the form of Comments anchored to the appropriate point in the story using Word's Track Changes feature. According to the *PaperSpecs* story, two employees at Melcher proceeded to write out the marginal text by hand on tracing paper, which was then scanned and color-corrected in Photoshop. The files were then passed to HeadCase Design in Philadelphia, where the building of the book began. The marginalia was immediately converted into layers for the master InDesign file. The colors, which had been painstakingly corrected once already in the scans, had to be color-corrected yet again. "The pencil just didn't look enough like pencil anymore," comments Paul Kepple at HeadCase. "So we'd have to do layer adjustments to adjust the colors to look like they were supposed to look." Moreover, the marginalia also had to be laid out in order to ensure that they remained proximate to the correct locale in the *Ship of Theseus* text, while ensuring that the book itself retained its standard industry dimensions, thus explaining the generous margins we see. The pages themselves, meanwhile, were also being artificially aged and distressed with yellowing. Yet more InDesign layers accrued. The result was that the size of the files ballooned enormously, making them unwieldy to open, transfer, and store.

And yet, even as the InDesign layers accumulated and the byte count swelled, the printed pages of *S.* are irreducibly flat. There is no indentation or embossment from the press of Eric's pencil point, no raised ridges of ink to trace beneath our fingers. The halftone screen that supports the age effects layered onto the paper hovers just on the threshold of detection by the naked eye. There is a real sense, then, in which even a mildly attentive reader cannot help but to acknowledge the artifice of *S.*'s production, not just from a commonsensical understanding of the circumstances of its making but from the constancy of page after page of sensory feedback. Nor is this exclusively a phenomenon in the visual register: as *PaperSpecs* noted, the cloth cover is printed on an imitation canvas known as Arlin, or artificial linen. The visible texture of the weave was then printed onto the white Arlin stock from a scan. "So the actual cover has a texture," comments Kepple, "but what you're seeing there is really printed." Indeed, running one's finger over the boards yields the sensation of texture, but not necessarily the texture one would expect from the cover's appearance.

What I earlier termed the suspension of disbelief thus becomes a key emblem of this instance of bookish media: *S.* is not a book; it is tangible media produced and designed to behave like a book, right down to the synthetic fabric dressing its boards. In that sense there perhaps *is* an argument for identifying it as a "blook," but I prefer to think in terms of what we might call secondary materiality, after Walter Ong's notion of secondary orality. Like secondary orality, which Ong famously glosses as electronic culture's more deliberate and self-conscious manifestation of those traits common to orality, secondary materiality is, to adopt Ong's phrasing, "both remarkably like and remarkably unlike materiality."[34] Secondary materiality is not, to my mind, the abstraction or abnegation of materiality, but its transposition: that is to say, new materialities imposed by the exigencies of artificially representing some putatively authentic material particular.[35] The sway of secondary materiality is especially evident in the emerging critical literature around *S.*, where there is of course keen interest in the book's marginalia and inserts and paratexts, but the circumstances of its actual making are taken for granted. Apart from the branding information on the slipcase, the only acknowledgment of *S*.'s identity as a product that exists outside of its own storyworld is a text block on the inside back cover, with copyright and other publication information presented in literal fine print.[36] As a consequence, for readers and critics of *S*., attention to materiality is generally only brought to bear *within* the shared conceit established by the weather-beaten copy of Straka's *Ship of Theseus*. To do otherwise would break the metafictional frame, and so the materiality that commands our attention is precisely what I have just termed a *secondary materiality*.

Secondary materiality, like bookish media, is not a failure of some exactitude in science. It is not as if had the designers been just a touch more clever, the technology just a little more state of the art, the production values just a little more elite, then the illusion would have been complete. On the contrary: I believe *S*. depends on the reader's muted but persistent awareness of its being a simulation. Just as the slippage between the actual feel of the Arlin stock and its printed textures results in a subtle sense of disconnect, the secondary materiality of the design as a whole serves to reinforce the slippages and displacements inherent in its metafictional conceit—an effect perfectly consistent with the slippages that characterize *S*. from the moment we slip it from its slipcase to reveal Straka's *Ship of Theseus* and the moment that book is opened to reveal its riot of marginalia and inserts, some of which will, inevitably, slip out of the book and into the reader's hands. The confirmation is right there in front of us, in the title of the Straka novel itself. The *Ship of Theseus* refers us to Plutarch, specifically the parable wherein he asks whether a ship whose boards and beams have been systematically replaced by new timber until none of the original remain is in fact still the same ship. This theme is inaugurated in the opening sentences of the very first insert likely to (quite literally) fall into the reader's hands, a photocopy of a letter ostensibly from Straka to a film producer named Grahn, excoriating him for having the temerity to claim that one of his movies was an adaptation of one of Straka's previous novels: "It is true that you have retold many *events* contained in my novel . . . but you have failed completely to tell the *story*."[37] This insert is itself contained within the translator's introduction to *The Ship of Theseus*, written by F. X. Caldeira, who ruminates on the mystery surrounding Straka's true identity, which she compares to the controversies surrounding Shakespeare's authorship. Of course Caldeira herself, being a translator, is engaged in exactly the same kind of project as Grahn, replacing the text of the original novel (purportedly written in Czech) word by word, sentence by sentence, joist and plank by joist and plank. Has Caldeira succeeded in retelling the "story," or has she merely recapitulated the same sequence of "events"? Is the text still the same text?

But of course, *S.* is *not* a translation, not really. Outside of the metafictional frame of the book, we know, unambiguously, that it was written by Douglas Dorst, a novelist and creative writing professor at Texas Tech University, in standard American English. And like other of Melcher's productions, *S.* was printed in China. Printing in China is done, as we have seen, to control costs (even with the added expense of overseas shipping, the margins are exceedingly favorable). But the efficiencies are more fine-grained than just those of the presswork. Each of the several dozen inserts in the book is manually placed at a prescribed page opening by a member of the Chinese labor force at the printing plant, executing what is known in the industry as "handwork"—one insert at a time, one copy at a time. This is a "digital" production of the truest and most fundamental kind, and the expense would be prohibitive in any other labor market. Indeed, Melcher has developed a reputation for enhancing its books with inserts: *New York Collapse* is replete with them (referred to as "removable artifacts"), as is *Mr. Robot*, which features something even more unique. One interior leaf from *Mr. Robot* has been torn from its faux Mead-style notebook and folded back in to the pages. There was no way to automate this part of the workflow, so each page of each copy had to be manually ripped out, folded, and inserted back in. Thus, elsewhere in the volume, one can locate the stub of the torn-away page still adhering to the binding; and the edges will fit together.[38] As with any of their projects, Melcher routinely spends time overseas ensuring quality control; in this instance, its staff also provided a schematic "tear guide" to ensure a baseline of consistency. Even so, no two copies of *Mr. Robot* will be exactly alike. Otherwise, however, the handwork that elite clients purchase permits no more variation than the industrial presses. This is evident in the final assembly spec sheet for *S.*, a document in the passive voice that is in fact a compact algorithm, complete with a subroutine, dedicated to ensuring that the book's complex, literal *digital* fabrication is performed without error: "Ephemera is placed inside book between specific pages as instructed below. Book with all ephemera inserted is then placed in slip case. Shrinkwrapped. 8 copies per carton."[39]

The extreme specificity of the fabrication process is itself a symptom of the medial status of contemporary book production. Because a book can nowadays be made out of almost anything, choosing to make it out of some select set of components (to the exclusion of others equally available in the global supply chain) is a medial act, rendering the codex form a platform or vector for a specific set of media effects. Just as Kamau Brathwaite realized his Video Style through pull-down menus of fonts, we nowadays build books layer by layer in tools like Photoshop and InDesign and we print them through a global production system wherein none of the pieces are beyond the reach of a project with adequate financing, and no production detail exceeds the tolerances for handwork in the Asian labor markets. In the case of *S.*, the coffee franchise napkin is in fact the most precarious item in the supply chain owing to there being but a single, sometimes inconstant vendor for the necessary paper stock.[40] What makes a book bookish media, then, is that it is a well-defined configuration of material components, with each component fully specced and specified according to a calculus of costs, sustainability, and creative vision. If, in some hypothetical future, that sole vendor for the napkin in *S.* was to disappear and a new paper stock substituted as the material support for the content entangled in its fibers by a four-color printing process, would *S.* still be the same book? This, I submit, is one of the few bookish questions Abrams and Dorst and the dazzling creative teams at Melcher and HeadCase do not want us to ask.

But this too is still only half the story. Like Zeno's arrow or perhaps the layers of an InDesign file, the sites of secondary materiality seem infinitely divisible. Just as Doug Dorst is the *Ship of Theseus*'s author, J. J. Abrams is *S.*'s auteur. Abrams, of course, is the director of blockbuster films in the *Star Wars*, *Star Trek*, and *Mission Impossible* franchises. At least up until *The Force Awakens*, however, his best-known work may have been *Lost*, which aired for six seasons on ABC beginning in 2004. *Lost* tells the collective and intertwined stories of dozens of survivors of a commercial airliner crash, marooned on a South Pacific island. *Lost* is also the series that, in the eyes of many, brought so-called transmedia storytelling into the mainstream. Transmedia has been glossed by Henry Jenkins and others as the practice of telling a story across multiple media platforms, with each platform or installment contributing a unique or distinct progression of the narrative.[41] It is thus not to be confused with adaptations or tie-ins, or what we call a novelization (a retelling of the same story in a different format). The *Blair Witch Project*, which began accruing a cult audience with a web site launched a full year before the film hit theaters in 1999, is often regarded as one of the earliest exemplars of transmedia storytelling, but the phenomenon quickly became both more complex and more mainstream, notably through the evolutions of *The Matrix* franchise and then Abrams's *Lost*. *Lost* incorporated not only the network TV broadcast of the show, but also the subsequent digital distribution of each episode via iTunes as well as so-called mobisodes (shorts produced for smartphone consumption), alternate reality games, video games, novels, and more, all collectively making up what is referred to as the show's storyworld or "expanded universe." One cannot truly say they have exhausted the *Lost* storyline without encyclopedic consumption of them all. Today, transmedia is a recognized form of storytelling and content distribution, incorporated into nearly ever mass-market entertainment franchise to some degree. Bookish media is thus one narrow band in the wider spectrum where Abrams operates. "People are drawn to J. J. Abrams for the fully realized worlds he creates," said one book industry insider. "Any project that manages to capture that in book form will appeal to his legions of fans."[42]

Though there were early hints and teasers circulating on the internet beforehand, *S.*'s transmedia deployment did not begin in earnest until just prior to its October 2013 publication date. First came "transmissions" broadcast from an NTS Internet radio channel dubbed "Radio Straka," which debuted more or less simultaneously with the initial publication of the work.[43] Then, on Friday, November 22, as part of a live Twitter chat being conducted from the Apple Store in SoHo in New York City, Abrams offered a cryptic series of clues and communiques. A reader had asked (only a month after the book's debut) if there was anything "major" left to discover. Abrams, via his Bad Robot Twitter account, replied: "There is quite a lot of 'hidden' things online. . . . I will give a clue to anyone who cares . . . TEN."[44] These tweets were quickly pounced upon by fans, who began enumerating possibilities and scenarios. Within a week, speculation had narrowed to the idea that there was more than one version of chapter 10 in the printed copies of the *Ship of Theseus* (in the book, chapter 10 is revealed as a pastiche of text by both Straka and Caldeira, with alternate versions alluded to). For a time nothing else happened. Then, in April of the following year, prominent bloggers in the *S.* community began receiving mysterious parcels containing the alternate endings. These, of course, were immediately scanned and shared online.[45] Dorst himself, meanwhile, tweeted a link to one that had popped up on the Tumblr site belonging to "Jen Heyward," the character who appears in the margins of the novel.[46] Populating real-world media platforms with fictitious projections from the storyworld is a common transmedia tactic: *S.*'s expanded universe also consists of multiple Twitter accounts, including ones for both the Jen and Eric characters (who tweet back and forth to one another, thus further extending the dialogue begun in the margins of the book), and several other authorized web sites, which are registered under independent domains and run by individuals who themselves become actors in the story.[47] These in turn have become jumping-off points (rabbit holes or trailheads in the parlance of transmedia) for additional plots derived from the *S.* storyworld. One of these, for example, concerns the mysterious Santorini Man, who first made his debut in a Radio Straka transmission.[48]

With all these different online elements, coupled with the fan activity that unfolds across blogs, tweets, and other online forums and channels, one might expect the boundaries of what is and isn't part of the work to become muddled. *S.* thereby enacts an eager textual scholar's "best" worst-case scenario.[49] In fact, however, as is common in transmedia franchises, these boundaries are rigorously policed by the fans themselves, who adjudicate so-called canon vs. non-canon installments and contributions. Those that are officially released by the producers of the franchise and contribute story elements that must be accounted for in any subsequent developments are sanctified as canon.[50] Nonetheless, from the standpoint of the bibliographical history of *S.*, the vast torrents of fan conversation and contributions must all be appraised as part of the reception of the work. All this is to say nothing of the online traces of *S.*'s acknowledged creators, Abrams and Dorst, whose appear-

12 | A page from a fan site devoted to *S.* showcasing the extent of a reader's bibliographical investigations. Note also the link to the "Radio Straka" site on right. Screenshot by the author from http://sfiles22.blogspot.com/2014/03/some thing-or-nothing.html.

ances are followed and documented, not least because they may, as we have seen, release additional clues, intentionally or otherwise.

It is hard to overstate the degree of seriousness and attentiveness that *S.*'s fans or self-styled "Searchers" bring to their efforts. For example, one blog post, several months before *S.*'s publication, identifies an otherwise cryptic trailer video posted to J. J. Abrams's Bad Robot YouTube channel as connected to the book based on the following evidence: "The font used for the caption at the end of the video appears to be the same as the one used on the original promotional banner at the Book Bloggers Conference in Book Expo America."[51] Clearly bookish media like *S.* are not compromising bibliography's habits of mind but actively cultivating and instilling them, training a wide range of readers to function much as bibliographers do. Fans, for example, have curated a resource documenting the correct placement of the inserts, essentially performing the work of professional catalogers; likewise, there is a page collecting bibliographical details of Straka's other eighteen "novels," intimations of the complete oeuvre gleaned from passing mentions in notes and annotations to *The Ship of Theseus*.[52]

What do S.'s readers do? They compile enumerative and descriptive bibliographies, they track down variants, collate texts, collect versions, adjudicate Apocrypha, archive ephemera, and seek out unique copies of the work—all of this across a myriad of different platforms, services, and networks. Moreover, they do so with the fervor typical of fan communities, with little tolerance for wrong information, baseless assumptions, and the botched presentation of evidence.[53] What will the bibliographical enterprise look like amid the torrents of the bitstream? I think I have some idea, but the Searchers of S. seem already to know.

Coda | The Postulate of Normality in Exceptional Times

A rainy morning, and a colleague and I arrive at the Houghton Library at Harvard. Unlike my visit to the Firestone Library at Princeton, I am not coming as a patron. My colleague and I are there as part of a project working to develop a suite of open-source software tools called BitCurator. We are meeting with a team of archivists to read data from a stack of floppy disks that once belonged to John Updike, whose papers the Houghton collects. In a ground floor room, droplets streaking the window, I sit and watch as the small red LED lamp on an external 3½-inch floppy drive flickers, the decades-old bits from what Jason Scott once called "poor black squares" (or think once more of Shannon's blank box) passing through the sensors in its read/write head, interpolated by firmware, sifted through a WriteBlocker (a component to ensure no cross-contamination between devices), and reconstituted in the form of a disk image, a perfect virtual surrogate. As the LED blinks, the drive mechanism makes soft whirring sounds, soothing as the sound of the rain on the sill. Wolfgang Ernst wrote of a similar flickering lamp, the magnetic recording light that pulsed as Milman Parry recorded the folk songs of the Serbian *guslari* singers: *archaeography*, or the archive writing itself was how Ernst glossed the moment.[1] The lamp flickers on and off. Something, nothing. Memory, oblivion.

Later, going through the logs generated by the imaging process, I notice something curious. Updike, I knew, had been a selective and spare computer user. He was a relatively early adopter, acquiring a Wang system in 1983 and keeping it for a decade before moving on to an IBM PC clone. He used these almost exclusively for word processing, abstaining even from email.[2] Yet several of the disk images from the Windows-era machine contain artifacts associated with the Macintosh operating system, a computer type I have no record of Updike ever owning. How did they get there? The diskettes, which bear labels written in Updike's own hand, had come directly from him, and no one had accessed them in the interim. Updike, I also knew, had dismissed his typist upon acquiring the Wang, and I had seen no mention of anyone ever taking the typist's place as a personal assistant. A friend or family member who was helping out? Possibly. Or had Updike in fact gotten a Mac late in his life? Again, certainly possible, though as we have seen he was a man who tended to stick with what he knew and trusted. A conversation with a confidante shed no additional light. What is incontrovertible is that at *some* point certain of the files on some of these diskettes were copied to and/or from a Macintosh. Whose and under what circumstances we do not know, nor do we know what other digital traces of Updike's writing life that Macintosh might contain.

Or maybe it would all be a proverbial wild goose chase. Maybe the traces and artifacts I had found were just bugs, or the byproduct of random blips of the microchip—after all, who knows why computers do some of the things they do? Maybe it was the work of a prankster designed to confound just such an e-paleographer as myself. Maybe there was a vast conspiracy afoot to obscure the fact that Updike ever owned a Mac, which I had unwittingly stumbled upon. Such musings, of course, are increasingly silly and extreme. But they also demonstrate the persistence of a problem that has challenged bibliographers for as long as there has been bibliography, namely the nature of bibliographical evidence.

The postulate of normality is a precept popularized (if that is the word) by Fredson Bowers in the middle of the last century. It states that when examining a hand-press book or other early printed matter, one must never assume that some particular feature or artifact is the result of anything other than normative presswork unless and until one can provide absolutely compelling evidence to the contrary. In other words, the postulate is telling us we should accept that what we see is there for a rationally explainable reason. It is not there because the compositor was inebriated or inept or was seeking to sow chaos. All these things are possible of course, but the tyranny of their potentiality cannot be allowed to forestall the application of sound bibliographical judgement. Without such a postulate, Bowers concludes, "no laws of bibliographical evidence could exist, for the unknown human equation could successfully 'explain' any abnormality observed."[3]

Bowers frames the question as one of inductive versus deductive reasoning. Inductive reasoning permits extrapolating general statements from the summation of individual cases whose collective evidence, barring the extraordinary, all points to a common explanation. Inductive reasoning thus proceeds from the specific to the general. It allows for the possibility of new evidence that might overturn old, but the postulate itself is fundamentally conservative: it imposes a high barrier to corrections.[4] It is also, in its way, tautological: "normality" is what has already been normalized as normal. By contrast, deductive reasoning, championed by Bowers's great antagonist Donald F. McKenzie, begins with a hypothesis or conjecture, and then examines individual cases to confirm or refute it. Far from being selective or capricious in this regard, deduction adopts a posture of radical skepticism, repeatedly using the evidence it gathers to challenge its initial conjectures, iterating and reformulating and accepting of "knowledge" only as ever partial and contingent and subject to ongoing revision. "The nature of 'normality' so far revealed by historical evidence suggests that the 'norm' comprised conditions of such an irrecoverable complexity," wrote McKenzie, that the very idea—*normality*—"misrepresents the nature of the printing process," whose conditions "were extraordinarily complex and unpredictable."[5] In other words, there was nothing "normal" about printing or the people who printed; the normality that Bowers espoused existed only in his own thoughts, or, as the title of McKenzie's famous attack has it, in the phantasmagorical works of shades, "printers of the mind."[6]

This distinction between inductive and deductive reasoning is the precipice between something and nothing, memory and oblivion. It is the fulcrum for what we believe we know and can know about a past to which none of us enjoys complete or direct access. And it is an epistemological schism that has marked my writing throughout this book. The kind of access to the past that computers and digital media afford is sometimes intoxicatingly specific and particular: tracked changes date- and time-stamped down to a millisecond, the potential to collate these with a browser history captured on the same computer, the ability to mine hundreds or thousands or hundreds of thousands of files for patterns and correlations, the potential for traces of the most minute user behavior lodged deep within the recesses of the operating system—all these suggest that the heritage of the bitstream has the potential to yield vast dividends, of a scale unprecedented in literary history. (Such possibilities also illustrate the imperative for the highest ethical standards around privacy and personal information.) Whereas it might take scholars such as Lawrence Rainey their whole career to amass the evidence with which to elucidate the dates of *The Waste Land*'s composition, a scholar working with a cache of born-digital manuscript evidence might do the same in minutes or hours or days or weeks, exposing, in the process, an extraordinary web of connections among aspects of a writer's life, at least in so far as they are gathered and collected in the alter-ego of that writer's computer.

And yet, we have also seen how elusive knowledge of the past (even the very recent past) can be. Instead of tracking their changes, writers may choose to overwrite the same document again and again, preserving little beyond the final state of their text. Updike, meanwhile, died only a decade ago, and many who knew him and were close to him are still alive and available; but the question of the Macintosh has gone unanswered. The same is true of Kamau Brathwaite and details of his software and systems. To some extent this is likely a symptom of casual disregard. Computers, being consumer devices marketed in accordance with the dictates of planned obsolescence, subject to routinized cycles of upgrade and replacement, always on the verge of being edged out by the new and the next, offer little encouragement to attend to their specificity. (How many of us could itemize a complete inventory of our own hardware and software over the last twenty or thirty years?) Questions about such things can also seem weirdly obsessive or intrusive, as if one were inquiring about the subject's preferred make and model of food processor instead of their word processor.

But these may not even be the right questions. In stark contrast to Brathwaite, a complete emulation of the desktop environment of one of Salman Rushdie's early Macintoshes has been available to patrons in the reading room at the Rose Manuscript, Archive, and Rare Book Library at Emory University since 2010—but it has yet to produce a major scholarly breakthrough.[7] Indeed, it is not obvious that the bibliographical challenges created by the use of computers in literary production are fully or even frequently compatible with those confronted by traditional analytical bibliography. They can be, in some very particular instances—the example of *Beloved*'s digital and physical manuscript materials, say. But this may prove to be the exception, with the future of "e-paleography" for a poet such as I described in the introduction lying instead with data mining, machine learning, and the quantum modeling of agency and causality.

We know that text, in the sense of human-readable output created at the behest of human intention and agency, accounts for only the barest fraction of the data a computer's operating system generates, even for the most mundane of tasks. This is the lesson of a 2013 artist's book entitled *Diff in June*, a five-pound, seven-hundred-page volume recording and printing every item that changed on a single day on a single computer's hard drive. The project's originator, Martin Howse, describes it as "a novel of data archaeology in progress tracking the overt and the covert, merging the legal and illegal, personal and administrative, source code and frozen systematics."[8] It is, in other words, a data dump. The folio-sized pages consist almost entirely of seemingly arbitrary strings and numerals and punctuation, printed without interruption or break in tiny 6 pt. type. Here too then is Ernst's archaeography, the archive writing itself. Like other books of its kind—it bears comparison to Warhol's *a, A Novel* and Kenneth Goldsmith projects like *Traffic* and especially *Day*—*Diff in June* is not a book for reading. In this it is a kind of limit case for what Carlo Ginzburg once termed venatic lore, every sign full of portent and intention but (here) foreclosing any and all attempts to trace them back to a point of origin.

Computers, as I have argued consistently throughout my writing, are distinguished not by virtue of their supposed immateriality but by virtue of their being material machines conceived and built to sustain an *illusion* of immateriality—the illusion itself being an artificially engineered and irreducibly material contrivance. This is the essence of the Turing machine, which aspires to be a universal model of well, *anything*, realizable through the simple additive actions of digits in a manner all but impossible to arithmetically compromise. The degree to which computers have succeed at propagating this illusion accounts for many of the casual desktop (and nowadays palmtop) miracles of our everyday: backspacing to correct a typo without leaving a trace, sending an email or "text" around the world in the blink of an eye, copying files without fear of their corruption.[9] Computers, we might say, are the one textual environment in which the postulate of normality is unassailable. There is *always* a rational explanation. Even a computer's random choices are never—as is known—truly random. The textual traces captured in *Diff in June* may be inscrutable, but they are never merely arbitrary. All of them are purposeful.

Of course computers are also never truly infallible. In 1994, the computing world was rocked by news of a hardware bug in some of Intel's new Pentium processor chips, with an estimated one in nine billion mathematical operations yielding an incorrect binary result. Though the impact on most users would have been imperceptible, the story nonetheless captured the public imagination and received widespread media coverage. A computer was outright and objectively *wrong*, owing to a defect in one of its parts. But the notoriety of the Pentium bug also speaks to the scarcity of such occurrences.[10] Most "bugs" are in fact code proceeding to a perfectly correct logical outcome that just so happens to be inimical or intractable to the user or to other elements of the system. The Y2K "bug," for instance, was code executing in ways that were entirely internally self-consistent, however much havoc the code was once expected to wreak.

The moth famously extracted from the relays of Harvard's Mark II mainframe in 1947 by Grace Hopper was a literal pest clogging up the works. Most bugs, however, result from a combination of human fallacy and the unimaginably complex permutations of logic chains deep within the arithmetically abstract innards of a system. (An ERROR message, as any computer user knows, always carries with it an implicit rebuke; not my error but *your mistake*, is what the machine seems really to be saying to us.) This is the premise of Ellen Ullman's 2002 novel, *The Bug*. Ullman is herself a programmer, and her novel is in part a loving recreation of that culture in its commercial infancy in the 1980s. The titular bug, which bears the name UI-1017 (its technical designation) and soon enough also "the Jester" (its personification), is a persistent but untraceable flaw that repeatedly but seemingly inconsistently and unpredictably crashes the software system the novel's cast of characters is contracted to deliver. It quickly consumes their attention and energies. Eventually, the Jester is traced to a one-pixel error by a programmer in an interface subroutine, which in turn spawns an uncomputable value when the mouse pointer samples the null space the error inscribes.

What is interesting to us here is the extent to which the debugging that Ullman portrays—a mostly mental exercise that comprises much of the action of the novel—is (again) a venatic process. "I turned to the release notes SM Corp. had sent along with the code changes," Berta, the narrator (and Ullman's stand-in), tells us. "Twenty-five dense pages of technical minutiae. Weeks passed during which time I followed many baffling trails deep into the arcana of operating systems. I began reading the release document the way Ethan had run his debugger: obsessively, every time I had a moment, over and over the same words to see if something would reveal itself."[11] Substitute one arcana for another—baffling trails for entrails—and we are back to what Ginzburg called *divinatio*, watching and waiting for mysteries to reveal themselves.[12] Such discipline is necessary because, as Berta tells us, a computer is built to do only one thing: to *run*. "It doesn't care about being understood," she elaborates. "It is a set of machine states—memory contents, settings of hardware registers—and a program, a set of conditions that determines how to go from one state of the machine to the next. Nothing unfolds from anything else. Nothing is implied. Nothing is connected. Under certain conditions, events go one way; if not, they go another. You're here; or else you're here, each 'here' discrete from every other." She adds: "*To a machine, all here's are equal.*"[13]

For all its technical preoccupations, *The Bug* is a deeply humanist text. Humans, it wants to reassure us, are not machines; *we* are *not* capable of functioning in a space where all here's are equally and arbitrarily available, at least not for long. The seeming susceptibility of machine states and formal logic to the caprice of the external human lifeworld eventually drives one of the novel's programmers—Ethan, a committed rationalist obsessed with mathematician John Conway's *The Game of Life*—to suicide. When Berta takes over and finally tracks down the error—not just the offending digit but the reason *why* it was capable of producing such destructive consequences—she makes clear that what is at stake is not just a technical victory. It is an epistemological vindication. "Because the world suddenly felt right again," Berta exults. "Human, bounded, knowable. We did not live surrounded by demons. There were no taunting jesters, no vexing spirits. We live in a world of our own making, which we could tinker with and control. I had never felt such a sense of command in my whole life: I know how this thing *works*, I thought, how it works for real and to the bottom. I know how the actual, physical world—a mouse moving across a pad—is seen by the code, how the program turns dumb pixels into windows and buttons and menus, anything we humans want them to be."[14]

What she is describing, of course, is normality. But the real lesson of *The Bug* is that such normality is possible *only* in the artificially induced interior logic of the machine. The rest of the world is messy, relentlessly analog (as opposed to digital) in Ullman's dichotomy; but the machine is, or should be, ruled by logic and reason. When it appears not to be, the consequences for our outlook on the world outside of its monadic space can be devastating. The price of normality is the world of here and here and here described by Berta, a world of discrete states and endlessly coequal paths. The price of normality is also, for Berta's programmer colleague Ethan, his life.

Bowers, in outlining his postulate, acknowledged that pressmen were not "robots," a striking enough image to conjure for an Oxford audience in 1959.[15] He was as much as saying that compositors were not computers, a necessary admission to guard against what would have been an obvious objection even then. Nonetheless, Bowers clearly believed most presswork was routinized (and therefore knowable) most of the time, in ways that ultimately align with the programmers' view of the computer systems in *The Bug*. By contrast, McKenzie concluded a decade later by despairing that even the science of what he termed "cybernetics" could fully comprehend the complexities of all the different variables and relations involved in presswork and the day-to-day operations of a printing house.[16] Strikingly then, Bowers and McKenzie each appealed to their own respective formulations of the highest kind of abstract artificial reasoning of their day (robotics and cybernetics) to make the case that bibliography operated on different terms—for McKenzie qualitatively so, while Bowers acknowledged only a difference of degree, not kind.

But if both Bowers's inductive reasoning and McKenzie's deductive method seem to ultimately possess a certain sameness—less tyrannosaurus and pterodactyl grappling on the edge of a primordial cliff than a snake eating its own tail—it is because both are in fact forms of inference. What Bowers and McKenzie both had in common was a vested interest in the assessment of bibliographical knowledge. But inference, as Kari Kraus notes, is a kind of "cognitive leap" from the known to the unknown. Whether the leap is ultimately conservative (inductive) or expansive (deductive) is less important than the crossing of the void between.[17] ("Void" here is a crude stand-in for any number of better words: working, thinking, sweating, agonizing, weighing, evaluating, sorting, sifting, parsing, judging, discriminating, comparing, evaluating, and so on.[18]) Moreover, according to Kraus, "*inference* is not a monolithic category but can be further subdivided into inductive inference, deductive inference, abductive, intuitive, probabilistic, logical, etc."[19] Induction and deduction were themselves often conflated in popular parlance, most famously by Sir Arthur Conan Doyle: Holmes's signature displays of "deduction" were in fact examples of *induction* as it is commonly defined, the elucidation of fuller truths from partial bits of evidence. But the two were used interchangeably in Doyle's day, both as synonyms for what we would identify as *inference*.[20] Inference brings us back again to Carlo Ginzburg and the "evidentiary paradigm" he perceives as the great epistemological counterweight to Galilean science.

For Ginzburg, who reads the venatic tradition through Conan Doyle, Freud, and especially the art historian Giovanni Morelli, the essence of inference is in the certainty that "infinitesimal traces permit the comprehension of a deeper, otherwise unattainable reality."[21] Thus, Conan Doyle's set pieces of "deduction" (induction), Freud's slips and dreams, and the incidental details of paintings upon which Morelli based his attributions. Beyond these figures from Western European intellectual history, though, Ginzburg reaches back to Mesopotamian divination and, ultimately, to the archetypal image of a hunter squatting on the forest floor, scanning for tracks and droppings, for broken branches and trampled leaves. This is, as I have argued previously, the same impulse that led Stephen Greenblatt to famously declare his desire to speak with the dead; it is what I termed at the time a forensic imagination, a particular amalgam of obsessive, excessive hypermediated detail (which is where forensics comports with the New Historicism— what Greenblatt and Catherine Gallagher term foveation), locality, and specificity, coupled with a belief in the power of storytelling and faith in our capacity for projection.[22]

As we saw in Chapters 1 and 2, scholars from Saidiya Hartman to Lisa Lowe have embraced aspects of this speculative or conjectural way of knowing—Hartman, whose critical fabulation is introduced out of necessity for the violences perpetuated by colonial archives of slavery, and Lowe out of a similar desire for a "conditional temporality," one that acknowledges "the existence of alternatives and possibilities that lay within, but were later foreclosed by, the determinations of the narratives, orders, and paradigms to which they gave rise."[23] These mandates for speculation take us beyond the mere adjudication of evidence, whether deductive or inductive. Kraus, meanwhile, demonstrates the extent to which the seemingly narrow and empirical domain of textual criticism has long been a safe harbor for just such sallies of the subjunctive.[24] And in book history at large, calls for feminist interventions in bibliography and print studies have sought to move scholarship away from the mere reclamation and recovery of female figures and instead to spaces of alternate possibility not accommodated by existing canons and archives.[25]

Against such thinking—it would seem—stands the digital computer, in all its Turing-complete, self-contained yet somehow universal embrace. Computers, as Ullman showed us, are not much for potentiality, only ever for a deterministic *now*: here or here or here or here, but never (possibly, just maybe) *there*. And yet, the nature of digital systems admits that nearly all access to the fundamentals of computation—beyond what we see in pixels on the screen or what we may hear as audio—is bound to be inferential, even speculative and conjectural.[26] Pixels themselves are just a brilliant prism for the shadows of computation, heres and heres and heres and heres that resemble shapes and images in the aggregate. But there are no fuller and more substantial things behind those shadows, just as there is no "bitstream" coiled inside the carapace of my laptop and no ones and zeros coursing through the chute of my cable modem (to come spraying forth if the line were cut). All this terminology ("bitstream," "cyberspace," "ones and zeros") is figurative, holding space for an epistemological encounter with what are (again to return to Kittler) ultimately only and ever voltage differentials.

The polymathic scholar Douglas Hofstadter has likewise confirmed the general trajectory of Ginzburg's intellectual history, bringing it into the present moment by arguing that much of science proceeds by recasting inference as direct observation, via various forms of instrumentation and technology:

> Today, for instance, ultrasound allows us to see a fetus moving about inside a mother's womb in real time. Note that we feel no need to put quotes around the word "see"—no more than around the word "talk" in the sentence "My wife and I talk everyday on the phone." When we make such casual statements we don't for a moment consider the weirdness of the fact that our voices are speeding in perfect silence through metallic wires; the reconstruction of sounds is so flawless and faithful that we are able to entirely forget the fact that complex coding and decoding processes are taking place in between the speaking mouth and the listening ear. . . . If, fifty years ago, high-frequency sounds had been scattered off a fetus, there would have been no technology to convert the scattered waves into a vivid television image, and any conclusions derived from measurements on the scattered waves would have been considered abstruse mathematical inferences; today, however, simply because computer hardware can reconstruct the scatterer from the scattered waves in real time, we feel we are directly observing the fetus. Examples like this—and they are legion in our technological era—show why any boundary between "direct observation" and "inference" is a subjective matter.[27]

Hofstadter goes on to prompt that, "much of science consists in blurring this seemingly sharp distinction."[28] This dynamic as much as any other accounts for our experience of the bitstream.

As I write this, for example, I am tracking rain cells over suburban Maryland using online Doppler radar available from dozens of different apps and sites (I have a leaky window seam and am wondering whether I'll need to get out some towels). Note that unlike Hofstadter's example of the sonogram, the colored blobs I see on the Doppler do not, in any mimetic sense, resemble rain. Yet not only do I accept the Doppler images as an accurate depiction of the weather conditions in my area (and thus a reliable predictor of whether or not I'll need to mop up), I also tend to regard what I am seeing as simply rain (*without* quotes) and not as an artificially enhanced visualization of the prevailing atmospheric conditions. Though I appreciate that the Doppler display is exactly that, the truth is that my understanding of what rain *is* has sufficiently expanded as to allow images produced by radar waves reflected from bands of precipitation to sit within the same referential horizon as the puddles I know will eventually appear on my windowsill.

In just the same manner, the bitstreams responsible for the image of the cat I'm looking at in my Twitter feed do not, in any mimetic sense, look like a cat. They don't look like anything at all, at least not until they are interpolated by firmware as signals whose waves (as we said at the outset) are as individuated as any majuscule. The image of the cat is a projection, an extrapolation, a computation. The same holds true for *any* phenomena on our screens, from video game avatars to the text of a text message—everything that ultimately reaches our eyes is a calculation, abstracted (paradoxically) as ever more arbitrary renditions of symbolic values that have their ultimate expression in magnetically coded flux reversals, electrostatic charges, or other idiosyncratic forms of inscription. Even the instrumentation that allows us to "see" the bits on the surface of a hard drive is fundamentally interpretative and interpolative, stochastically reconstructing an array of values much as the technology of the sonogram reconstructs the scatter of sound waves.[29] (The proposition to the contrary circumscribed the whole original cyberpunk fixation on "jacking in," that narcotic and narcissistic fusion of the brain's neuronal structures and the computer-generated abstractions of what William Gibson was the first to call cyberspace—the ecstasy and oblivion immanent in our encounters with the virtual.)

Computers as we know them are compact, exquisitely realized compressors for routinizing this oscillation between inference and observation, and accelerating it to what is experienced as instantaneous—continually refreshed and renewed through the kind of routines documented by Wendy Chun. They are not the first such technology to do so of course; the telephone, as Hofstadter says, the telegraph, and arguably writing itself all did the same. But computers are the first to do so in such a way that the illusion of immateriality—and normality—is broadly and consistently sustainable. The actual architecture of how this happens means we have no direct access to the data we depend on. The bitstream is only ever discoverable relationally. Bibliography of the born-digital proceeds from the inference that attends all historical knowledge, even as it acknowledges the fundamentally arbitrary and discrete nature of computation—a kind of epistemological Mobius strip realized in and through the torqueing conduits of the bitstream and its material circumstances.

The examples in this book demonstrate that it is at the threshold *between* the formally idealized state machine of the digital computer and the messy, human, and asymmetrical lifeworld of the people who use them that bibliography must center its investigations. Put plainly, people do weird, unexplainable stuff with computers all the time, and all the data dumps in the world—365 days of diffs—won't get us any closer to total recall. The future of digital literary heritage will be as hit and miss, as luck dependent, as fragile, contingent, and (yet) wondrously replete as that of books and manuscripts. It will be found in floppies that have sat dormant in shoeboxes under beds and in file systems from long-expired accounts. It will be in frayed power cords and recondite connectors, and it will be in chance interactions and serendipitous encounters and conversations. It will be in friendships and animosities. It will be in libraries and archives, but also data centers and server farms. It will be in search engines and feeds and torrents, in forks and commits, in scrapes and patches and builds, in Zooms and texts and Slacks and chats. It will be in human as well as machine memory. There will be enough of it, and there will be too much (yottabytes, perhaps), and all of the most precious parts will still be missing, or so it will always seem. The future of digital literary heritage will be what we make it out to be. Or it will be, if we can make a place in the world for this work.

It is October 2017 and I am back in Philadelphia a year and a half after the Rosenbach Lectures, this time for the Rare Book School's Bibliography Among the Disciplines conference, where I have been asked to deliver some remarks as part of the panel at the closing plenary. I have been awed by the range of topics, methods, and expertise in the sessions, from quilts and manuscripts to books and bindings to buildings and Bob Dylan CDs. Many of the presenters are early career scholars. I catch myself thinking: *bibliography is as big as the world*. But that is not the summation of the conference. There are also at-capacity pop-up sessions on the intersect of social justice and, yes, bibliography. There are urgent undercurrents on Twitter. As the speaker before me at the plenary notes, the audience for this event is still too homogeneous, and there is still too much anxiety over what is really *real* bibliography—and who gets to lay claim to doing it.[30] Meanwhile, all of us at the venue on Chestnut Street are struck by the disparity between our measured proceedings and the world beyond, still only a glimpse of what was to come as I write this now, in the summer of 2020, which may or may not be the last summer of Donald Trump's America. So when it was time for my closing remarks at the conference in 2017, I say: "Bibliography is as big as the world, but the world is bigger than bibliography." I add: "Anyone plugged into their social networks or the cable news back in their hotel room knows what I mean."

The previous month Hurricane Maria had torn across Puerto Rico, killing (by official estimate) nearly three thousand people; an unknown number more would die from cruel and calculated neglect in the months that followed. In California wildfires were burning, the most destructive the state had ever seen (they would be until the next year's, which would be worse, and 2020, which has proved the worst of all). These same fires furnished the cultural heritage community with the incredible image of the Getty Center complex silhouetted against hillsides glowing orange from the approaching inferno. And then there was the surreal trauma of Las Vegas's Mandalay Bay mass shooting (just two weeks prior), punctuating the everyday reality of gun violence in America—even as "law and order" exacted its ongoing and implacable and disproportionate toll. George Floyd, Breonna Taylor, and Elijah Mc-Clain were all still alive, but Freddie Gray, Eric Garner, and Tamir Rice were already gone. And, at a bus stop on my own campus the previous spring, a young Black man, 2nd Lieutenant Richard W. Collins III, newly commissioned in the United States Army and just days from graduating from nearby Bowie State University (a HBCU) with his bachelor's degree, had been murdered by a white University of Maryland student for refusing to step off a sidewalk and into the gutter.[31]

I give voice to all these things at the plenary. But I know what my audience knows, that I am their least essential messenger. I feel I need to say something more, something that has to do with bibliography (because I too admit the anxiety of imposter syndrome). My thoughts turn to another conference note I have scratched on my pad: *what bibliography offers is an uncompromising commitment to the individuality of all things, every instance, every copy.* I don't remember what session or paper prompted that thought. Maybe it was the one on Craven Ord's brass rubbings, or maybe it was watching a computer-imaging scientist virtually "unroll" the withered sheets of a two-thousand-year-old scroll shriveled into an undifferentiated lump of carbon. That which had previously been opaque became transparent in the blink of a pixel; the illegible became legible; oblivion became memory. I say it out loud: "What bibliography offers is an uncompromising commitment to the individuality of all things, every instance, every copy."

Such a commitment takes discipline. Often it also takes certain forms of expertise, the kind that help you recognize a folio in sixes when you see one. These are habits of mind, coupled with access to training and material resources (like libraries and archives). But the truth is you don't need bibliography to appreciate the uncompromising individuality of things. A beat-down (I can only imagine) will focus the attention pretty good that way too, lying stretched out in the gutter, cheek pressed against the pavement, pebbles in the asphalt looming large as boulders, quartz and mica and bits of broken glass filling the field of vision. Or the terrible specificity of curbsides, a swell of concrete poured at some particular day and time, worn since by weather and feet and wheels. That curbside and all its everyday imperfections— that one and not this one—sometimes becomes the line between life and death, as it did for the young Black man on my campus who made the decision not to step off. There is nothing bibliography has to offer that is as uncompromising as that. It is a *here* of the ultimate consequence.

Bibliography may be as big as the world, but the world is bigger than bibliography. Even as one's world may one day contract to curbsides and pavement. What bibliography can offer is a practice, a committal, an ethos. Not only to recognize individuality amid extremity, but to do so in a way that admits diachronicity into the aperture of our engagements: diachronicity, history, and memory—even or especially conditional or conjectural memory—and rememory—so that the present becomes a palimpsest. One could always start (again) with McKenzie and his oft-repeated conviction that "bibliography. . . can, in short, show the human presence in any recorded text."[32] But we must also and especially see and cite the work of the new generation of bibliographers and textual scholars, who are remaking our imagination of what bibliography is and can be in light of the reality that the "human" itself has been a historically contested and repressive category.[33] As Brigitte Fielder and Jonathan Senchyne affirm in the introduction to their groundbreaking collection *Against a Sharp White Background: Infrastructures of African American Print* (the volume itself titled after Zora Neale Hurston's declaration, "I feel most colored when I am thrown against a sharp white background"), "this work has crafted itself alongside the backdrop of a predominantly white field that has necessitated the additional labor of working against existing structures of exclusion and erasure while also producing the innovative creative work, conversations, and methodological practices of African American print culture."[34] Black marks on a white page, then, but also a poured concrete curbside—or the Formica lunch counter, the vinyl bus seat, or the barbed wire and the watchtowers. And the history of a campus that was built, wholly or in part, by the labor of enslaved persons on land colonized from an indigenous people, the Piscataway Conoy. As the University of Maryland historian Ira Berlin has noted, "If slaves didn't lay the bricks, they made the bricks. If they didn't make the bricks, they drove the wagon that brought the bricks. If they didn't drive the wagon, they built the wagon wheels."[35] This is a bibliographically minded statement. It is also what I mean by the diachronicity of our entanglements, and it is why I make space for *these* actual facts in the final pages of a book about bibliography (carrying the dedication that it does).

Bibliography is about a commitment to individuality, but it must also be a commitment to collectivity. To the modulation between the this and that, the now and then, which are themselves *always* between the here and here and here. The bitstream is one particular technological form—currently pressing and present—that this modulation and entanglement takes. It will inflect our archives and our memory, of that there is no question. But all things are as exceptional as our perception of our own current times—and have always been. Bibliography is simply a way of naming what comes after that self-assured sentence. It is a disciplinary hedge, or maybe just a poor practical shim, against the complacency of norms. It is a habit of mind and a habit *to* mind.

Notes

Preface

1. R. J. Morris, "Electronic Documents and the History of the Late Twentieth Century: Black Holes or Warehouses," in *History and Electronic Artefacts*, ed. Edward Higgs (Oxford: Clarendon Press, 1998), 33.

2. In A Room of One's Own *and* Three Guineas, ed. Morag Shiach (Oxford: Oxford University Press, 2008), 296–97.

3. This episode (which dates from June 2016) was widely reported. See http:// www.newyorker.com/culture/culture-desk/why-did-google-erase-dennis-coopers -beloved-literary-blog. Following a legal wrangle, Google restored the deleted data: https://www.facebook.com/permalink.php?story_fbid=1114019298684536 &id=214073142012494.

4. Amy Hungerford has enumerated these concerns in their rawest form, and they are as fraught with contingency and circumstance as they have ever been: when the rent goes up, when a grant or a job is lost, and when "love or friendship or illness or birth or prejudice" manifest. See Hungerford, *Making Literature Now* (Stanford: Stanford University Press, 2016), 17. It may well be that these imponderables continue to exert far greater influence over prospects for what I am terming literary heritage than any of the topics I treat here. See also Simone Murray, *The Digital Literary Sphere: Reading, Writing, and Selling Books in the Internet Era* (Baltimore: Johns Hopkins University Press, 2018).

5. See Kirschenbaum, "Operating Systems of the Mind: Bibliography After Word Processing (The Example of Updike)," *PBSA* 108.4 (2014): 412.

6. See Kirschenbaum and Sarah Werner, "Digital Scholarship and Digital Studies: The State of the Discipline," *Book History* 17 (2014): 425. More recently, Whitney Trettien has begun developing a framework merging book history and media studies, relying on terms common to both: substrate, platform, interface, and format. See Trettien's "A Hornbook for Digital Book History," lecture delivered June 24, 2020, via Zoom for the Rare Book School: https://www.youtube .com/watch?v=YJh-WWrb3ow.

7. Aaron Pressman, "Ebook Reading Is Booming During the Coronavirus Pandemic," *Forbes* (June 18, 2020): https://fortune.com/2020/06/18/ebooks -what-to-read-next-coronavirus-books-covid-19/.

8. Kenya Evelyn, "Black US Authors Top New York Times Bestseller List as

Protests Continue," *Guardian* (June 11, 2020): https://www.theguardian.com /books/2020/jun/11/new-york-times-bestseller-list-black-authors.

9. The three lectures are available at, in sequence: https://www.youtube.com /watch?v=6TuA4dkRegQ, https://www.youtube.com/watch?v=XX4KstPpFa4, and https://www.youtube.com/watch?v=Wm_DuhVrhGM.

10. Dickey's poetry was published at the Internet Archive in September 2020. See https://archive.org/details/william_dickey_hyperpoems_volume_1 and https://archive.org/details/william_dickey_hyperpoems_volume_2.

11. See especially in this regard my oral history with Charles Bigelow, available both in transcript and video: https://archive.computerhistory.org/resources /access/text/2019/10/102738267-05-01-acc.pdf and https://www.youtube.com /watch?v=NkfWtxGwoZM.

12. See Kirschenbaum et al. *Books.Files: Preservation of Digital Assets in the Contemporary Publishing Industry* (College Park: University of Maryland and the Book Industry Study Group, 2020). Available at: https://drum.lib.umd.edu/han dle/1903/25605.

Introduction

1. See the account published in Rainey, *Revisiting* The Waste Land (New Haven: Yale University Press, 2005).

2. Ibid., 3.

3. Kirschenbaum, *Track Changes: A Literary History of Word Processing* (Cambridge: Harvard University Press, 2016), 7.

4. See Blair, *Too Much to Know: Managing Scholarly Information Before the Modern Age* (New Haven: Yale University Press, 2010), 6–7.

5. This is something of a mantra for Doctorow, repeated in many interviews and speeches.

6. An observation first tendered in 1996 by John Lavagnino in "The Analytical Bibliography of Electronic Texts." Available at: http://citeseerx.ist.psu.edu/view doc/download?doi=10.1.1.542.8899&rep=rep1&type=pdf.

7. Von Neumann's text is widely reproduced.

8. See Shannon, "A Mathematical Theory of Communication," *Bell System Technical Journal* 27 (July 1948), 380. Shannon's article was reprinted the following year as a monograph from the University of Illinois Press with a supplemental essay by his colleague Warren Weaver; this publication also changed the definite article in Shannon's title from "A" to "The."

9. Hansen, "Media Studies," in *The Routledge Companion to Literature and Science*, ed. Bruce Clarke and Manuela Rossini (London: Routledge, 2011), 358.

10. Kittler, "There Is No Software," *ctheory* (1995). The essay has been reprinted in various venues.

11. See Sadie Plant, *Zeros + Ones: Digital Women and the New Technoculture* (New York: Doubleday, 1997), 34–35. Plant further suggests that digital computers

reverse the usual binary, so that a zero (female, absence) signifies positively of presence or intent (as in the hole struck through a punch card), whereas a 1 (male, presence) signifies the absence of value (56–57).

12. See Chen, *Placing Papers: The American Literary Archives Market* (Amherst: University of Massachusetts Press, 2020). Chen writes: "The literary archives market does not support scholars, it feeds them. The distinction seems minute, but the difference is critical. Scholars are dependent on the market, not the market on scholars" (8).

13. McKenzie, "'What's Past Is Prologue': The Bibliographical Society and the History of the Book," in *Making Meaning: "Printers of the Mind" and Other Essays*, ed. Peter D. McDonald and Michael F. Suarez, S.J. (Amherst: University of Massachusetts Press, 2002): 269–270.

14. McKenzie, "The History of the Book," in *The Book Encompassed: Studies in Twentieth-Century Bibliography*, ed. Peter Davison (Cambridge: Cambridge University Press, 1992), 298.

Chapter 1

1. See Steedman, *Dust: The Archive and Cultural History* (New Brunswick: Rutgers University Press, 2002), 26–29. Steedman argues that an illness suffered by the historian Jules Michelet may have been brought about by his exposure to *bacillus anthricis* (anthrax), contracted by inhaling the spores of decaying paper and parchment—a literal case of archive fever.

2. For additional details of the process, see: https://blogs.princeton.edu/mudd /2015/08/toni-morrisons-born-digital-material/. For an introduction to digital preservation, see Trevor Owens, *The Theory and Craft of Digital Preservation* (Baltimore: Johns Hopkins University Press, 2018).

3. Although Word and WordPad are both Microsoft products, the DOS-based version of Word that Morrison's computer would have been running in the mid-1980s (almost certainly Word 2.0 or 3.0, released 1985 and 1986, respectively) is long out of date, and its version of the DOC file format is not supported by the company's current software. There are workarounds and conversion utilities, but all of them would have involved the installation of additional programs—not an option that was immediately available to me on the tightly controlled workstation in the reading room.

4. The specific *Beloved* files are: BLV302.DOC (labeled "BLV302 Reformatted as 1-120 / 1st draft type pages 302–401 / BELOVED / Section 3"), BELOVED2. DOC and BLV189.DOC (both on the same disk, labeled "BELOVED 2 / STORED AS BLV189 [starting at pg. 249] 2nd Draft typed pages 249–404 SECTION III"), BELOVED3.DOC (labeled "BELOVED3BK / BELOVED3.DOC / Typed pages starting at 405"), and BELOVED.DOC (labeled "SECTION I / BELOVED1bkp / BELOVED TYPED PAGES 1–248 EDITED CORRECTED 8/29/86.") Understanding an author's (and her assistants') file naming and labeling is an important

aspect of working with born-digital materials and illustrates the evidentiary value of handwritten labels and other accessories. In this instance, we can further confirm that the word processing program in question was MS-DOS Word because one of the sleeves of the diskettes is annotated with a handwritten directory path: C:\WORD\FILES87.

5. Caroline Rody is but one of the many readers to remark on the significance of the novel ending with its title word. See Rody, "Toni Morrison's *Beloved*: History, 'Rememory,' and a 'Clamor for a Kiss,'" *American Literary History* 7.1 (Spring 1995): 102, 113. Rody, not having the benefit of access to *Beloved*'s manuscripts at the time of the writing of her essay, proceeds with a reading of the text's closing lines unaware of their revision history.

6. Toni Morrison, "Home," in *The House That Race Built: Original Essays by Toni Morrison, Angela Y. Davis, Cornel West, and Others on Black Americans and Politics in America Today*, ed. Wahneema Lubiano (New York: Vintage, 1998), 6.

7. Ibid., 8.

8. Since my visit to Princeton, one additional diskette, unlabeled, containing two files with partial drafts of *Beloved*, has come to light. This item is identified as Disk 139 in the finding aid.

9. Automating such operations is currently a fertile but far from settled research space in computer vision science. For the current state of the field, see David A. Smith and Ryan Cordell, *A Research Agenda for Historical and Multilingual Character Recognition* (2018). Available online: https://ocr.northeastern.edu /report/.

10. Chris Hall, "J. G. Ballard: Relics of a Red-Hot Mind," *Guardian* (August 3, 2011).

11. See Chen, *Placing Papers*, 94–105.

12. Scott Neuman, "Internet Pioneer Warns Our Era Could Become the 'Digital Dark Ages,'" *NPR* (February 13, 2015).

13. For an overview of this early history, see Thomas Elton Brown, "The Society of American Archivists Confronts the Computer," *American Archivist* 47.4 (Fall 1984): 366–382.

14. F. Gerald Ham, "The Archival Edge," *American Archivist* (January 1975): 5–13.

15. See Pasquale, *The Black Box Society: The Secret Algorithms That Control Money and Information* (Cambridge: Harvard University Press, 2016).

16. See Viktor Mayer-Schönberger's *Delete: The Virtue of Forgetting in a Digital Age* (Princeton: Princeton University Press, 2011), Virginia Eubanks, *Automating Inequality: How High-Tech Tools Profile, Police, and Punish the Poor* (New York: St. Martin's Press, 2016), and Safiya Umoja Noble, *Algorithms of Oppression: How Search Engines Reinforce Racism* (New York: New York University Press, 2018).

17. My thanks to Jeffrey Moro and his dissertation-in-progress on "Atmospheric Media" for shaping some of my thinking about data centers and the environment.

18. James Bamford, "The NSA Is Building the Country's Biggest Spy Center," *WIRED* (March 15, 2012).

19. There are 1024 yottabytes in a brontobyte; and 1024 brontobytes in a geopbyte.

20. Jacques Derrida, *Archive Fever: A Freudian Impression*, trans. Eric Prenowitz (Chicago: University of Chicago Press, 1995), 90.

21. Steedman, 4.

22. Michelle Caswell, " 'The Archive' Is Not an Archives: On Acknowledging the Intellectual Contributions of Archival Studies," *Reconstruction* 16.1 (2016).

23. Steedman, 4.

24. Cook, "Electronic Records, Paper Minds: The Revolution in Information Management and Archives in the Post-Custodial and Post-Modernist Era," *Archives and Manuscripts* 22.2 (1994): 300–328. Importantly, Cook's essay sought to articulate connections between recent archival practice to what it termed "post-modern" theory.

25. Sterling, *The Hacker Crackdown* (1992). Electronic edition: http://www .gutenberg.org/files/101/101-h/101-h.htm. Emphasis in original.

26. The reference is to Gibson's canonical description of "cyberspace" in his novel *Neuromancer* (New York: Ace, 1984).

27. Sterne, "Out with the Trash: On the Future of New Media," in *Residual Media*, ed. Charles R. Acland (Minneapolis: University of Minnesota Press, 2006), 19.

28. See Sterling's "Dead Media Manifesto": http://www.deadmedia.org/mod est-proposal.html.

29. Sterling, "Delete Our Cultural Heritage," *Telegraph* (June 12, 2004).

30. Ibid. We should be careful not to romanticize this (often gendered) labor. As one archives professional made clear to me, the salaried expert Sterling proffers is an ideal; too often, the intensive work of processing collections is performed by underpaid (or unpaid) interns, students, or other categories of contingent employees who are statistically majority female.

31. All quotations of Urbach are from an internal Xerox PARC planning paper dated June 11, 1971, available here: https://archive.org/stream/pendery_papers /pendery_papers_djvu.txt.

32. See, for example https://spectrum.ieee.org/computing/hardware/why -the-future-of-data-storage-is-still-magnetic-tape.

33. Richard B. Gentile, "On the Reading of Very Old Magnetic Tape," *Datamation* (October 1973): 58.

34. As is clearly evident when reading through technical documentation for the TAR format: "Each file archived is represented by a header record which describes the file, followed by zero or more records which give the contents of the file. At the end of the archive file there may be a record filled with binary zeros as an end-of-file marker. A reasonable system should write a record of zeros at the end, but must not assume that such a record exists when reading an archive." See https://www.gnu.org/software/tar/manual/html_node/Standard.html.

35. See the SAA's definition of an archives here: https://www2.archivists.org /about-archives.

36. See https://www.lockss.org/.

37. Ernst, "Discontinuities: Does the Archive Become Metaphorical in Multi-media Space," in *Digital Memory and the Archive* (Minneapolis: University of Minnesota Press, 2013), 138.

38. Cook, 302.

39. From this point on, some readers may question the omission of Wolfgang Ernst, whose work on the media archaeological apparatus has been so essential to me in other contexts. (See, for example, my essay "The .txtual Condition," in *Comparative Textual Media: Transforming the Humanities in the Postprint Era*, ed. Jessica Pressman and N. Katherine Hayles (Minneapolis: University of Minnesota Press, 2013), 53–70. In my view, Ernst and Chun advance complementary and largely compatible accounts of the nature of digital memory, both emphasizing the degenerative and regenerative cycles of storage technologies. I have opted to follow Chun in this instance because her path through this terrain—proceeding as it does from Foucault's theories of biopolitics and a careful genealogy of twentieth-century models of human and machine memory alike—seems to me more germane to a discussion of *Beloved*, wherein memory is inseparable from the ways the body stores trauma and the body's scars are inscriptions of racialized violence.

40. Chun, "The Enduring Ephemeral, Or the Future Is Memory," in *Media Archaeology: Approaches, Applications, and Implications*, ed. Erkki Huhtamo and Jussi Parikka (Berkeley: University of California Press, 2011), 184.

41. Ibid., 192.

42. Ibid., 199.

43. Ibid., 192.

44. Jennifer Gabrys, "Telegraphically Urban," in *Circulation and the City: Essays on Urban Culture*, ed. Alexandra Boutros and Will Straw (Montreal: McGill-Queen's University Press, 2008), 49. I am grateful to Jussi Parikka's *A Geology of Media* (Minneapolis: University of Minnesota Press, 2015) for this reference.

45. Steedman, 164.

46. Quoted in Anthony Grafton, foreword to C. V. Wedgwood, *The Thirty Years War* (New York: New York Review of Books, 2005), x.

47. See Michael Marder, *Dust* (New York: Bloomsbury, 2016), 1–5.

48. One dramatic example: the recovery of a dozen new digital artworks from floppy disks belonging to Andy Warhol, created c. 1985. See the 2014 news release from the Carnegie Mellon team responsible here: https://www.cmu.edu/news /stories/archives/2014/april/april24_warholworksdiscovered.html.

49. Only in rare cases is the physical carrier integral to preserving the functional content of digital media. One noteworthy example comes from the games industry, where anti-piracy measures have been known to consist of intervention

in a diskette's low-level magnetic recording structures with the result that the game wouldn't work if copied from its original source.

50. Morrison, *Beloved* (New York: Plume, 1987), 35–36.

51. Rody, 101.

52. Morrison, *Beloved*, 36.

53. Marisa Parham, *Haunting and Displacement in African American Literature and Culture* (London: Routledge, 2009), 8. Parham's book (and much of her ongoing work) offers a literary and cultural genealogy of haunting, memory, and ghosts in the Black imaginary. See also, for example, her digital "pocket" *Black Haunts and the Anthropocene*: https://blackhaunts.mp285.com/.

54. Chun, *Programmed Visions: Software and Memory* (Cambridge: MIT Press, 2011), 167.

55. Ibid., 97.

56. In its seemingly inevitable collapse of fixed temporal categories, the digital archive might perhaps be taken as an instantiated model of the kind of "strategic presentism," recently surveyed by Wai Chee Dimock: "Unlike mainstream historicism, however, [strategic] presentism turns to the past not as a discrete object of knowledge but as a relational process, interactively generated through the connectivity as much as the gulf between two points of analysis." See her Editor's Column, *PMLA* 133.2 (March 2018): 260.

57. See Hartman's "Venus in Two Acts," *Small Axe* 22 12.2 (June 2008): 1–14. Of the archive's essential violence, Hartman writes: "Yet how does one recuperate lives entangled with and impossible to differentiate from the terrible utterances that condemned them to death, the account books that identified them as units of value, the invoices that claimed them as property, and the banal chronicles that stripped them of human features?" (3). The archive's temporal (and spatial) category collapse as a prerogative of the state is also the lesson of Gayatri Chakravorty Spivak's much earlier and important "The Rani of Sirmur: An Essay in Reading the Archives," *History and Theory*, 24.3 (October 1985): 247–272.

58. Several computer languages have moved to excise the vocabulary of "master" and "slave" from their internal lexicons, for example. See https://motherboard.vice.com/en_us/article/8x7akv/masterslave-terminology-was-removed-from-python-programming-language. See also the intervention of Black Digital Humanities, including the work of Kim Gallon, Jessica Marie Johnson, Marisa Parham, Catherine Knight Steele, and others. Johnson's "Markup Bodies: Black [Life] Studies and Slavery [Death] Studies at the Digital Crossroads," *Social Text* 36.4 (2018): 57–79, is exemplary in its melding of critical race theory's critique and technical rigor.

59. With regard to rememory and the locution "picture," it is perhaps helpful to know that archivists working with born-digital materials refer to the *image* of some particular piece of media; an image in this sense is not a photograph but rather an exact copy and surrogate—mathematically authenticated—of every bit

once stored on the original, in one long, linear sequence—in other words, a bitstream.

60. Morrison, *Beloved*, 275.

61. It is worth noting in this regard that the conservators at Princeton recovered each individual file from the original diskettes without altering their original date and time stamp. The retention of the original date and time stamps—so called MAC values, Modified/Accessed/Created—occlude the fact of the file's extraction from its physical source media. We thus encounter them without reflection of the reality of their ongoing migration across software and systems. To be clear, the original MAC values are essential metadata to have preserved, and this is no criticism—quite the contrary. But the consequence is that the institutional circumstance of the digital artifact is not visible as part of its own self-displayed history, which is to say as its rememory.

62. Karl Ove Knausgård, in book 5 of *My Struggle*, recounts something of the same way of thinking: "What the connection between the floppy disk and the screen was I had no idea; something had to 'tell' the machine that an 'n' on the keyboard would become an 'n' on the screen, but how do you get dead matter to 'tell' anything? Not to mention what went on when the letters on the screen were saved onto the thin little disk and could be brought back to life with one tap of a finger, like the seeds that had been trapped in ice for hundreds of years and then, under certain conditions, could suddenly reveal what they had contained all this time, and germinate and blossom." See Knausgård, *My Struggle: Book Five*, trans. Don Bartlett (New York: Archipelago, 2016), 396.

Chapter 2

1. Dickey, "A Ham Sandwich or Some Hay," *NER/BLQ* 10.1 (1987): 44.

2. Vidal, "In Love with the Adverb," *New York Review of Books* (March 29, 1984). This history is treated extensively in my *Track Changes: A Literary History of Word Processing* (Cambridge, MA: Harvard University Press, 2016). See especially chapter 3.

3. Among other reasons for not buying a computer, Berry offered that his wife does all his typing and copyediting for him.

4. Dickey, 45.

5. For more on Apple's design philosophy, see Lori Emerson, *Reading Writing Interfaces: From the Digital to the Bookbound* (Minneapolis: University of Minnesota Press, 2014), 76–85.

6. The commercial has been discussed many times, but the best critical treatment I know remains Ted Friedman, *Electric Dreams: Computers in American Culture* (New York: NYU Press, 2005), chapter 5. For IBM's "Tramp" campaign, see https://www.ejumpcut.org/archive/onlinessays/JC35folder/IBMtramp.html.

7. For background, see Michael A. Hiltzik, *Dealers of Lightning: Xerox PARC and the Dawn of the Computer Age* (New York: HarperCollins, 1999).

8. Talese, *A Writer's Life* (New York: Random House, 2006), 42.

9. See my oral history with Charles Bigelow, May 24, 2017, at the Computer History Museum for his memories of Reed and the Bay Area's arts and design community. CHM Reference number X8212.2017. Available at https://archive.computerhistory.org/resources/access/text/2019/10/102738267-05-01-acc.pdf as well as on YouTube: https://www.youtube.com/watch?v=NkfWtxGwoZM.

10. From a 2005 Stanford commencement address. Quoted in Niraj Chokshi, "The Trappist Monk Whose Calligraphy Inspired Steve Jobs and Influenced Apple Designs," *Washington Post* (March 8, 2016).

11. Dickey's poem is reproduced in a facsimile image of the festschrift here: https://www.reed.edu/calligraphy/reynolds-festschrift.html.

12. Dickey, "Poem Descending a Staircase," in *Hypermedia and Literary Studies*, ed. Paul Delany and George P. Landow (Cambridge: MIT Press, 1991), 145.

13. Dickey, "A Note on the Poems," *NER/BLQ* 10.1 (1987): 97.

14. Dickey, "The Mill and the Store," *NER/BLQ* 10.1 (1987): 107.

15. For more, see: https://retronauts.com/article/679/episode-126-a-deep-dive-into-hypercard-and-myst.

16. *HyperCard™ User's Guide* (Cupertino: Apple Computer, 1987), xvi.

17. Reprinted in "Douglas Adams on HyperCard" in *The Macintosh Reader*, ed. Doug Clapp (New York: Random House, 1992), 217.

18. Leonard Sanazaro, "Charting the Uncharted: William Dickey's Hypertextual Forays into the Future," unpublished essay in the Deena Larsen Collection at the Maryland Institute for Technology in the Humanities (University of Maryland College Park). Retrieved from Larsen's iBook laptop.

19. Dickey, "The Education of Desire," in *The Education of Desire* (Hanover: Wesleyan University Press, 1996), 68.

20. Dickey, "Poem Descending a Staircase," 149.

21. Ibid.

22. Ibid.

23. Letter from William Dickey to Deena Larsen (September 28, 1992) in Electronic Literature Archives (Washington State University, Vancouver).

24. Quoted in Kirschenbaum, "Editing the Interface: Textual Studies and First Generation Electronic Objects, *TEXT* 14 (2002): 37. Larsen's remarks are from her editor's introduction to the *Complete Electronic Poems of William Dickey*.

25. Though Eastgate is best known for work published with its proprietary Storyspace software, several of the titles in its catalog of "serious hypertext" were distributed as HyperCard stacks, including John McDaid's *Uncle Buddy's Phantom Funhouse* (1993) and Larsen's own *Marble Springs* (1993).

26. See Noah Wardrip-Fruin and Nick Montfort, eds., *The New Media Reader* (Cambridge: MIT Press, 2003). There is no mention of Dickey in the printed volume.

27. In addition to the CD-ROM for the *New Media Reader*, one HyperPoem, "Volcano," was self-published by Dickey in a small edition as a printed chapbook. My thanks to James Ryan for this information.

28. There is also a tranche of correspondence between Larsen and Dickey, Sanazaro, and others, including Eastgate's Mark Bernstein, on deposit at the Electronic Literature Lab at Washington State University, Vancouver. It does not shed any light on the reasons for Eastgate's ultimate failure to publish.

29. So-called emulation as a service: see http://eaas.uni-freiburg.de/.

30. The two volumes of Dickey's HyperPoems are accessible at https://archive.org/details/william_dickey_hyperpoems_volume_1 and https://archive.org/details/william_dickey_hyperpoems_volume_2. The erotica is contained in volume 2.

31. Jerome McGann, "The Gutenberg Variations," *TEXT* 14 (2002), 6.

32. Snodgrass, foreword, Dickey, *The Education of Desire*, xi.

33. Ibid., np.

34. Steven Levy, *Insanely Great: The Life and Times of Macintosh, the Computer That Changed Everything* (New York: Penguin, 2000), 188.

35. See John Scull and Hansen Hsu, "The Killer App That Saved Macintosh," *IEEE Annals of the History Computing*, 41.3 (2019): 42–52. For a more general overview of desktop publishing, see Frank Romano (with Miranda Mitrano), *History of Desktop Publishing* (New Castle: Oak Knoll, 2019). See also the two special issues of the *IEEE Annals of the History Computing* devoted to the desktop publishing industry, 40.3 (2018) and 41.3 (2019), both edited by Burton Grad and David Hemmendinger. Each contains invaluable firsthand accounts.

36. Robert Palladino's name is not to be confused with Palatino, a mid-twentieth-century typeface designed by Hermann Zapf which also became a popular early Macintosh font.

37. A PageMaker how-to manual included the tidbit that the *QE2* used the software to produce daily shipboard bulletins, much as ocean liners had carried their own printing presses in previous eras. "The news pages are put together into a PageMaker publication file in London, then transmitted by satellite to the luxury liner where a laser printer is used to print 1200 copies for the ship's passengers." See Tony Bove and Cheryl Rhodes, *Desktop Publishing with PageMaker* (New York: Wiley, 1987), xvi.

38. The reference here is of course to Eisenstein's still-indispensable *The Printing Press as Agent of Change* (Cambridge: Cambridge University Press, 1979).

39. Quoted in Jennifer Schuessler, "A Tribute to the Printer Aldus Manutius, and the Roots of the Paperback," *New York Times* (February 26, 2015).

40. Barbara A. Brannon, "The Laser Printer as an Agent of Change: Fixity and Fluxion in the Digital Age," in *Agent of Change: Print Culture Studies after Elizabeth L. Eisenstein*, ed. Sabrina Alcorn Baron, Eric N. Lindquist, and Eleanor F. Shevlin (Amherst: University of Massachusetts Press, 2007), 358. As the title of the essay and its venue make clear, Brannon is drawing an explicit comparison between the laser printer and desktop publishing and Gutenberg's introduction of movable type, as recounted by Eisenstein. Nonetheless, Brannon is careful to

insist: "The laser printer is no more single-handedly responsible for the current information revolution than was any one invention of Gutenberg's day: just as the printing press is commonly used as a metonymy for the whole of the print culture revolution, the laser printer was the gathering point for a number of associated technologies and it is used here as a shorthand for the digital revolution" (355).

41. Scull and Hsu, 51.

42. See Doris Monica Brathwaite, *A Descriptive and Chronological Bibliography (1950–1982) of the Work of Edward Kamau Brathwaite* (London: New Beacon Books, 1988).

43. Edward Kamau Brathwaite, *X/Self* (Oxford: Oxford University Press, 1987), 87.

44. Ibid., 85.

45. Kamau Brathwaite, "Dream Chad," in *DreamStories* (New York: Longman, 1994), 48.

46. Ibid., 49.

47. Ibid.

48. In *Ark* (New York: Savacou North, 1994), np.

49. There were several models of StyleWriter, first introduced in 1991. Brathwaite probably owned the original or its immediate successor, the StyleWriter II. The Apple StyleWriter was an inkjet printer, as opposed to the far more expensive laser printers typically associated with desktop publishing. As such, it was incapable (at least without some special accommodation) of handling the state-of-the-art PostScript fonts, which, being device independent, largely drove the desktop publishing revolution. Instead, Brathwaite would have had to rely on so-called bit-mapped fonts, which were essentially pictures of letterforms drawn pixel by pixel and stored in different point sizes. There was no "hinting" or other effects to smooth out their curves; if such a font was enlarged too much it would bristle in its appearance, becoming "jagged" in the manner characteristic of early computer displays and printouts. Like a number of artists and typographers, however, Brathwaite embraced the distinctive look.

50. Interview with Kamau Brathwaite, in *Talk Yuh Talk: Interviews with Anglophone Caribbean Poets*, ed. Kwame Dawes (Charlottesville: University Press of Virginia, 2001), 37.

51. See my pages on Brathwaite in *Track Changes* (2016), 197–203, 218–219. I have tried to avoid duplicating too much of the story I tell there here, but some overlap is inevitable (and essential).

52. Kamau Brathwaite, *MiddlePassages* (New York: New Directions, 1993).

53. I am grateful to Chuck Bigelow and Steve Matteson for their assistance identifying ꇙꀒꀒ.

54. Quoted by Antonio Cavedoni in Dave Addey, *Typeset in the Future: Typography in Science Fiction Movies* (New York: Abrams, 2018), 144.

55. For a detailed account of this work, see Alessandro Calizzi, "The Final Act at Nebiolo: The Quest for a 'Universal' Typeface," parts 1 and 2: https://articles

.c-a-s-t.com/forma-dattilo-modulo-nebiolos-last-efforts-to-produce-a-universal
-typefac-aa965dc0bb9f.

56. Addey, 146.

57. How or exactly when STOP got onto Brathwaite's computer, we cannot say absent access to the machine itself. It was not a font that would have come factory installed. But it (along with Eurostile and other Nebiolo designs) appears to have been widely available in bitmapped and PostScript formats. Brathwaite's copy of STOP could have come from a commercial font library he purchased, from a floppy disk passed along by a friend, or it could even have been downloaded from an early internet site (though there is no indication Brathwaite ever used a modem with his Mac). An inventory of the type library on Sycorax would be a fascinating undertaking if it were ever possible.

58. Letter from Epler to Brathwaite, March 19, 1993 (New Directions Publishing Corporation records, Houghton Library, Harvard College).

59. Ibid.

60. For a firsthand account of the difficulties involved in printing Brathwaite's work, see Graeme Rigby, "Publishing Brathwaite: Adventures in the Video Style," in *The Critical Response to Kamau Brathwaite*, ed. Emily Allen Williams (Westport: Praeger, 2004): 250–263. Rigby was editor of the British poetry newsletter *The Page*, which printed several of Brathwaite's SVS texts.

61. As described in a letter from Epler to Brathwaite, July 20, 1993 (New Directions Publishing Corporation records, Houghton Library, Harvard College).

62. See, for example, the Custom STOP group on Flickr, which invites contributors to publish photos of variations on the font: https://www.flickr.com/groups /customstop/

63. Kamau Brathwaite, *MiddlePassages* (Newcastle Upon Tyne: Bloodaxe, 1992).

64. See Bryant, *The Fluid Text: A Theory of Revision and Editing for Page and Screen* (Ann Arbor: University of Michigan Press, 2002).

65. As the correspondence between Brathwaite and Barbara Epler and other figures at New Directions will confirm, via the New Directions archives at the Houghton Library, Harvard University.

66. Email to author from Timothy J. Reiss, August 28, 2015.

67. Longman, University of Wisconsin Press, and Wesleyan University Press all printed books of Brathwaite's direct from his own manuscript, ideally an electronic copy transmitted on disk.

68. See Nelson, *Geeks Bearing Gifts: How the Computer World Got This Way* (Sausalito: Mindful Press, 2009), 128.

69. See Edmond, *Make It the Same: Poetry in the Age of Global Media* (New York: Columbia University Press, 2019), 20–61.

70. Rigby, 252.

71. *Ark*, np.

72. Per Timothy Reiss, a colleague and confidant of Brathwaite's at NYU.

73. Infante, *After Translation: The Transfer and Circulation of Modern Poetics Across the Atlantic* (New York: Fordham University Press, 2013), 163.

74. Ibid., 170.

75. The bitstream is thus also what passes from a computer to a printer in the transition from screen to page. The first digital type foundry was created in 1981 in Marlborough, Massachusetts. Its name: Bitstream Inc. Matthew Carter, one of its principals, describes the work: "Finally, a laser plotter, a machine which places very fine dots very accurately on film, is used to produce a complete page. A broadsheet newspaper page for example, which can be set in under two minutes; text type, display type, line-art, half-tone and scanned-in type are set at a single pass. There is no longer a distinction between type and illustration, between cast type and woodcut, between slug and engraving, and between galley and half-tone negative: these are now integrated in the RIP [Raster Image Processor], in the bitstream fed to the plotter and on the output film." See Carter, "The Digital Type-foundry," *Visible Language* 50.2 (August 2016).

76. Stewart Brown, "Interview with Kamau Brathwaite," *Kyk-over-al* 40 (1989): 84–93. Quoted in Stuart Brown, "'Writin' in Light': Orality-thru-Typography, Kamau Brathwaite's Sycorax Video Style," in *The Pressures of the Text: Orality, Texts, and the Telling of Tales*, ed. Stuart Brown, Birmingham University African Studies Series No. 4 (Birmingham: Centre of West African Studies, University of Birmingham, 1995), Kindle loc. 2823.

77. Ibid.

78. Funkhouser, "Chronology: *ConVERSations with Nathaniel Mackey* (We Press, 1999)," unpublished MSS.

79. Brathwaite, *DS (2) dreamstories* (New York: New Directions, 2007), 13, 154.

80. Ibid.

81. Brathwaite, "Dream Chad," 49.

82. Reprinted in Charles Bernstein, "95 Theses," *Profession* (October 2016). I hope Charles will indulge me my response here.

83. See W. W. Greg, "The Function of Bibliography in Literary Criticism Illustrated in a Study of the Text of *King Lear*," *Neophilologus* 18 (1933).

84. For more on the chronological overlap between bibliography and early information theory, see my *Mechanisms: New Media and the Forensic Imagination* (Cambridge: MIT Press, 2008).

85. See Viscomi, *Blake and the Idea of the Book* (Princeton: Princeton University Press, 1994). This form of scholarship as recreation or reenactment has a precedent in Brathwaite studies in an essay by Carrie Noland, "Remediation and Diaspora: Kamau Brathwaite's Video Style," in *Diasporic Avant-Gardes: Experimental Poetics and Cultural Displacement*, ed. Carrie Noland and Barrett Watten (New York: Palgrave 2009): 77–97. Noland develops a careful and persuasive reading of the Video Style and its relation to Brathwaite's earlier poetics of nation language; she then proceeds to describe a session with her own Macintosh in which she attempts to duplicate the spatial arrangement of one of Brathwaite's poems in

Microsoft Word, thereby demonstrating how line breaks and other features of the text were influenced and enforced by the software. But while Brathwaite *could* have used Word—it was available for the Macintosh during the period in question—there were other possibilities, like Claris's MacWrite II, that are equally plausible. (MacWrite II was in fact eclipsing Microsoft's market share right around the time Brathwaite got his Mac.) If Noland has a source for Brathwaite's use of Word, it is not mentioned in her essay. It matters because all word processors have their own distinctive behaviors and defaults. Moreover, we know nothing about what kind of Mac Noland herself was using, or what version of Word or how her tabs and system options were set; nor do we even know that Brathwaite composed and laid out the book in a word processor as opposed to, say, Aldus Page-Maker, then the standard for desktop publishing. I admire Noland's experiment very much, and the results she offers are compelling: indeed, she may have succeeded in furnishing an explanation for certain formal qualities of the poem in question. My point here is not to chide her the lack of documentation but to point to the limits on critical knowledge that obtain whenever we operate amid a horizon of uncertainty as regarding a writer's or artist's hardware and software.

86. Contrast this lacunae with a page from a HyperCard textbook written by one of William Dickey's colleagues at San Francisco State University utilizing a screenshot of his poetry as an illustration; the caption to the screenshot cites the specific clip art libraries, typefaces, and icons that are visible. See Stephen Wilson, *Multimedia Design with HyperCard* (Englewood Cliffs: Prentice Hall, 1991), 10.

87. Joseph A. Dane, "Meditation on a Composing Stick," in *Blind Impressions: Methods and Mythologies in Book History* (Philadelphia: University of Pennsylvania Press, 2013), 146.

88. Matt Cohen, "Time and the Bibliographer: A Meditation on the Spirit of Book Studies," *Textual Cultures* 13.1 (2020): 201.

89. Ibid., 189.

90. Ibid., 190.

Chapter 3

1. Sven Birkerts, *The Gutenberg Elegies: The Fate of Reading in an Electronic Age* (Boston: Faber and Faber, 1994), 117–118.

2. Houston, *The Book: A Cover-to-Cover Exploration of the Most Powerful Object of Our Time* (New York: W. W. Norton, 2016), xv.

3. Ibid., xvi, xvii.

4. *The Book* includes a colophon with some of these details; others can be obtained from the paratext.

5. Asia Pacific Offset was the successor of a prior company, Mandarin Offset, founded in 1971 by British publisher and book magnate Paul Hamlyn. Offset, of course, refers to the mode of printing that these firms deliver for their clients; the

lingering Orientalism, however, is a window onto a long, fraught history of colonialism and bookmaking descending from Hong Kong's status as a British Crown colony and its ties to the London book trade. Mandarin itself was a subsidiary of Hamlyn's Octopus Publishing, which had first pioneered the use of Chinese labor to print illustrated books for the Western marketplace in the 1960s. With Mandarin, he introduced a model wherein the firm procured paper, ink, and other supplies, then rented time on presses throughout southeast China (using the onsite labor force, of course), while also managing the logistics of packaging and shipping the finished books to clients. All this was done at margins that wouldn't have been possible anywhere else in the world. This history contributes to the prevalence of illustrated printing in Asian markets today (details from my interview with Derek Freeman, former chairman of Mandarin Offset, August 9, 2018).

6. See Darnton, "What Is the History of Books?" *Daedalus* 111.3 (1982). In "The Digital Publishing Communications Circuit," *Book 2.0*, 3.1 (2013), Padmini Ray Murray and Claire Squires update Darnton to account for developments such as the rise of literary agents, self-publishing platforms, digital publishing, and e-reading devices. On supply chain logistics, see Miriam Posner, "See No Evil," *Logic Magazine* 4 (April 2018) and Deborah Cowen, *The Deadly Life of Logistics: Mapping Violence in Global Trade* (Minneapolis: University of Minnesota Press, 2014). For a discussion of supply chain logistics in relation to contemporary bookmaking, see Kirschenbaum, "Bibliologistics: The Nature of Books Now, or a Memorable Fancy," *Post45* (April 8, 2020): https://post45.org/2020/04/bibliologistics -the-nature-of-books-now-or-a-memorable-fancy/#footnote_2_11526.

7. For an extended discussion of the implications for publishers' archives and future book history, see Kirschenbaum et al., *Books.Files: Preservation of Digital Assets in the Contemporary Publishing Industry* (College Park: University of Maryland and the Book Industry Study Group, 2020): https://drum.lib.umd.edu/handle/1903/25605.

8. Fiona Raven and Glenna Collett, *Book Design Made Simple: A Step-by-Step Guide to Designing and Typesetting Your Own Book Using Adobe InDesign*, Second Edition (Vancouver: 12 Pines Press, 2017), 2.

9. "A Day in the Life of . . . a Book Designer," September 4, 2017. Available at https://readingagency.org.uk/young-people/003-skills/a-day-in-the-life-of-a-book -designer.html.

10. Lisa Maruca, in the conclusion to a book juxtaposing the bodies of workers with "bodies of type," has made a similar point: "The nuts and bolts and plastic of the machine on your desk have disappeared, along with their connection to real human bodies. Who made it? Where? Erased from this picture are the modern-day equivalents to John Dunton or Joseph Moxon's Master Printer, those who create software, whom we might more fruitfully consider our collaborators. These workers and their products, after all, allow us to write—we do not make the text ourselves." See Maruca, *The Work of Print: Authorship and English Trade Texts, 1660–1760* (Seattle: University of Washington Press, 2007), 171.

11. For an account of a specific logistical software regimen, see Miriam Posner on SAP, "The Software That Shapes Workers' Lives," *New Yorker* (March 12, 2019).

12. Luna, "Books and Bits: Texts and Technology 1970–2000," in *A Companion to the Book*, ed. Simon Eliot and Jonathan Rose (Chichester, West Sussex: Wiley-Blackwell, 2009): 381.

13. See "The Artist-Novelist: Douglas Coupland on Canada, Culture, and His Hybrid Practice," *Artsy* (October 21, 2013): https://www.artsy.net/article/editorial-the-artist-novelist-doug-coupland-on-canada-culture. "I was lucky," Coupland comments. "I learned Quark in 1988—I got in early."

14. Douglas Coupland, "I Luv Helvetica," *New York Times* (August 27, 2006): https://coupland.blogs.nytimes.com/2006/08/27/i-luv-helvetica/.

15. Douglas Coupland, *Microserfs* (New York: HarperCollins, 1995), 110.

16. I am grateful to my Ph.D. student Dr. Brian Davis for introducing me to several of these authors. See Davis's dissertation, *Books as Archives: Archival Poetics in Post-1980 Experimental Writing and Book Design* (University of Maryland, 2020).

17. See https://www.theverge.com/2015/6/9/8660703/mark-danielewski-interview-the-familiar-house-of-leaves. Here Danielewski narrates: "We just finished Volume 2 [of *The Familiar*], and there is now this kind of informal [production company] Atelier Z where people are really working. The entire act structure of Volume 2 is mapped out, all the graphics were being tracked. We had various walls pinned with the chapter splash pages, tracing the graphics, the rainstorm, seeing the progression of how the words were being incorporated into those designs, what those words were." As of this writing there are seven volumes of *The Familiar* published, with plans for future installments on hold.

18. See Mindell Dubansky, *Blooks: The Art of Books That Aren't* (self-published, 2016); Nicholson Baker, "Books as Furniture," in *The Size of Thoughts: Essays and Other Lumber* (New York: Random House, 1996), 182–203; and Garrett Stewart, *Bookwork: Medium to Object to Concept to Art* (Chicago: University of Chicago Press, 2011). Dubansky catalogs objects that *look* like books (hence "blooks") but serve other functional purposes—for example, a book that is really a flask (to hold one's liquor), or a purse, or a carapace for an alarm. Baker, in his essay (originally written for the *New Yorker*), is interested in the use of books as room décor and props, a trend that appears to be ever on the rise twenty-five years later. Stewart's "bookwork," finally, is the name he gives to books and accumulations of books that become gallery pieces—sculptures or installations built on the raw form of the book as a shape and an icon. In *How to Do Things with Books in Victorian Britain* (Princeton: Princeton University Press, 2012), meanwhile, Leah Price surveys like phenomena through a specific historical epoch (it turns out that Victorian readers did all manner of things with their books besides read them). My interest in bookish media owes a debt to all these scholars and researchers but is distinguished by its attention to the material (medial) conditions of contemporary bookmaking, what I have also elsewhere termed bibliologistics.

19. See Pressman, "The Aesthetic of Bookishness in Twenty-First Century Literature: Steven Hall's *The Raw Shark Texts*," *Michigan Quarterly Review* 48.4 (2009) and *Bookishness: Loving Books in a Digital Age* (New York: Columbia University Press, 2020). In her essay, Pressman identifies bookishness as a post-year-2000 novelistic phenomenon, one tied to nostalgia and mourning for the book; it is, specifically, "the fetishized focus on textuality and the book-bound reading object." In her more recent monograph of the same title, Pressman expands the purview of bookishness beyond the literary to encompass a variety of different kinds of objects—a laptop case designed to look like an old book for example, in the manner of a blook; or a bed's headboard made out of books (books as furniture); as well as the bookwork of artists such as Brian Dettmer and Doug Berube; as Pressman says, "once you recognize bookishness, you see it everywhere" (1). She also delineates what is at stake in the *-ishness* of bookishness, tracing the etymology of the suffix to its Old English roots in national identity to suggest the term addresses "subject formation through relationality" and the activity of "locating and identifying a community of subjects in physical and spatial contexts" and even the physical proximity of "objects that rub off on us" (10). My own emphasis on bookish media represents what might be taken as an almost inverted account, one that sees books as increasingly aligned and subsumed by other media types—at the technical and logistical (if not always aesthetic and affective) level. In my account, as homology with other media types increases, books become merely book*ish*, their historical and material dimensions and distinctions flattened (if not effaced). The sense of nearness connoted by the traditional, slightly pejorative use of bookish (the suspicion of being just a little *too* close to books, as Pressman says) is also perhaps salutary here: bookish media as the uncanny valley of bookishness.

20. Simone Murray has completed a textbook entitled *Introduction to Contemporary Print Culture: Books as Media*, forthcoming in late 2020 from Taylor & Francis. It presents an overview of contemporary publishing and its relation to other sectors of the media sphere. I lacked the benefit of Murray's book while writing this chapter, but it promises a more systematic survey of some of the industry dynamics alluded to here.

21. Andrew Clarke, interview with author, July 10, 2018.

22. See Levinson, *The Box: How the Shipping Container Made the World Smaller and the World Economy Bigger* (Princeton: Princeton University Press, 2006).

23. Pool, *Technologies of Freedom* (Cambridge: Harvard University Press, 1983), 23.

24. Gates, *The Road Ahead* (New York: Penguin Books, 1996), 129.

25. Kittler, *Gramophone, Film, Typewriter*, trans. Geoffrey Winthrop-Young and Michael Wutz (Stanford: Stanford University Press, 1999), 4.

26. Jenkins, *Convergence Culture: Where Old and New Media Collide* (New York: New York University Press, 2006), 15.

27. See Pressman, "Jonathan Safran Foer's *Tree of Codes*: Memorial, Fetish, Bookishness," *ASAP/Journal* 3.1 (January 2018): 97–120 and Jones, *The Emergence of the Digital Humanities* (London: Routledge: 2013), 155–156.

28. See my "Books After the Death of the Book," *Public Books* (March 31, 2017). Available: https://www.publicbooks.org/books-after-the-death-of-the-book/.

29. See Cramer, "What Is Post-Digital?" in *Postdigital Aesthetics: Art, Computation, and Design*, ed. David M. Berry and Michael Dieter (London: Palgrave Macmillan, 2015): 12–26. Cramer comments: "the term 'post-digital' can be used to describe either a contemporary disenchantment with digital information systems and media gadgets, or a period in which our fascination with these systems and gadgets has become historical" (13). While many might regard the return to books as an instance of the former, it is in the latter sense that I use the term here.

30. See their website at https://melcher.com/about-us/. In 2012, Melcher founded the Future of Storytelling, an annual invitation-only industry event dedicated to digital platforms and experiences.

31. I don't wish to create the impression this approach is unique to Melcher and HeadCase. The conceit of a book appearing as if it were a much older book, an artifact from another time that descends to readers' hands after a long and difficult journey, did not, of course, originate with their productions. An obvious predecessor I have written about extensively is *Agrippa: A Book of the Dead*, the collaborative artist's book produced by Kevin Begos Jr. in 1992 with contributions from William Gibson and Dennis Ashbaugh (see *Mechanisms* and http://agrippa .english.ucsb.edu/). In the mass market, an early example is Brian Froud and Terry Jones's "facsimile" of *Lady Cottington's Pressed Fairy Book* (1994). Perhaps all of this work descends from the nineteenth-century German artist Carl Maria Seyppel's *Mumiendrucke* (mummy prints), books whose pages were processed with techniques for artificial aging that Seyppel patented in 1882 (my thanks to Bethany Nowviskie for this example; see https://blogs.lib.unc.edu/rbc/2016/12/08/mummy -printing-in-the-rare-book-collection/). Finally, as Andrew Ferguson notes to me, all of these techniques owe a debt to centuries of technical innovation by forgers and hoaxers. Today there are many books on the market that adopt this aesthetic, particularly in the milieu of children's and young adult literature as well as video game and film tie-ins. A systematic survey would be of much interest.

32. While doubtless some customers may feel genuinely deceived, other such notes may be instances of so-called shit-posting: intentional derailing with vacuous, misleading comments.

33. See Aaron Berman, "The Most Complex Project of 2013?" Parts 1 and 2, *PaperSpecs* (December 10, 2013, and January 7, 2014): https://www.paperspecs .com/caught-our-eye/s-by-jjabrams-complex-project/ and https://www.paper specs.com/caught-our-eye/s-by-jjabrams-complex-project-2/. Details and quotations in this paragraph and the next are sourced from these articles.

34. Ong, *Orality and Literacy: The Technologizing of the Word* (London: Routledge,1982), 136.

35. The secondary materialities of *S.*—manifest in its palpably flat pages or the synthetic cloth weave—are, in their own way, not dissimilar from the trade-offs subsequent generations of printers would make in reproducing the famous marbled page in the first edition of *Tristram Shandy,* whose individuation as a result of the paper marbling process is flattened by photo-reproductive technologies, often rendering it black and white in the process.

36. For just one example, see Emma de Vries and Yra van Dijk, "'Book for Loan': *S.* as a Paradox of Media Change," in *Book Presence in a Digital Age,* ed. Kiene Brillenburg Wurth, Kári Driscoll, and Jessica Pressman (New York: Bloomsbury Academic, 2018): 127–144. Arguably the only acknowledgement of *S.*'s primary (as opposed to secondary) materiality in this otherwise fine essay is in a credit to Mulholland Books for permission to reproduce a photo.

37. Abrams and Dorst, *S.* (New York: Little, Brown, 2013). Insert.

38. There is a precedent for this in *RAW* issue 7, a comic book published in 1980 that came with its top right-hand corner ripped away and with another, randomly selected top right-hand corner taped back into the book; see https://www.comics.org/issue/358764/. My thanks to Lee Konstantinou for this example.

39. *S.*'s spec sheet is courtesy of Melcher's production director Susan Lynch.

40. My thanks to Susan Lynch for this detail.

41. Jenkins, *Convergence Culture,* 95–96.

42. Quoted in Logan Hill, "A Long Time Ago, in a Universe More Analog," *New York Times* (October 27, 2013).

43. See http://www.radiostraka.com/ and https://www.mixcloud.com/NTS Radio/radiostraka-show1/.

44. @bad_robot, Twitter (November 22, 2013).

45. The (currently) five alternative endings are collected here: https://whoisstraka.wordpress.com/chapter-10-alternative-endings/. Only one is identified as "authorized."

46. The tweet reads: "Straka's original ending found?" @dougdorst, Twitter (April 3, 2014). The "Jen Heyward" Tumblr site is https://jenheyward.tumblr.com/. On July 9, 2014, Dorst tweeted the link again, "ICYMI."

47. The Jen and Eric Twitter accounts are @JenTheUndergrad and @EricHusch. Each follows only the other. See also @VMStraka and @FXCaldeira (the latter follows the former, but not the other way around).

48. At http://www.eotvoswheel.com.

49. If *S.* is the textual scholar's best worst-case scenario, it is the cataloger and librarian's *worst* worst-case scenario. Different libraries have adopted different policies around the circulation of *S.*, with some keeping it confined to the rare books room—a decision that has the side-effect of nullifying the presumed ontology of the book as a circulating library copy! The University of Pennsylvania has, unsurprisingly, done a particularly good job with its cataloging, enumerating every insert and its placement: https://franklin.library.upenn.edu/catalog/FRANKLIN_996125 6213503681. Finally, *S.*, by mere virtue of its title, is a search engine's worst-case

scenario. The title for the Amazon listing was eventually changed to *Ship of Theseus*.

50. For example, https://whoisstraka.wordpress.com/other-s-resources/.

51. "Stranger Video," *S.Files22* (August 27, 2013): http://sfiles22.blogspot.com /2013/08/stranger-video.html.

52. See http://sfiles22.blogspot.com/2013/01/list-of-inserts.html and http:// sfiles22.blogspot.com/2013/01/srtraka-bibliography.html [misspelling of Straka's name in URL is *sic*].

53. For an extended example, see http://sfiles22.blogspot.com/2014/03 /something-or-nothing.html. This entry on a fan-run site begins, "A few hours ago @CannongateBooks tweeted this picture with the accompanying words of 'Page twelve, line two, word seven' It [the tweet] is a copy [image] of page 12 and on that page the second line word seven is 'something'. The poster then compares the image of the page tweeted by @CannongateBooks (a British bookseller) to their own copy and concludes they appear to be identical, but that "lots of analysis on this page needs to take place to uncover something we may have missed." The poster then updates the entry: "we have had another tweet by @Cannongate-Books – 'Page 327, line 21, words 4 and 5' If I can count correctly this gives us 'is coming.'" At this point the pattern is clear. The rest of the posting consists of further tweet page/line/word references alongside scans of the relevant text from the book for confirmation. Eventually (and perhaps anti-climactically, though maybe not for a fan) the message is revealed to be notice of the availability of signed first editions of *S.* from the seller, Cannongate. The fastidiousness with which the unfolding real-time evidence is documented—as well as the initial supposition that it may have been pointing to variant copies in circulation—is illustrative of the strong bibliographical sensibility among *S.*'s readership.

Coda

1. See Ernst, "Media Archaeography: Method and Machine Versus History and Narrative of Media," in *Media Archaeology: Approaches, Applications, and Implications*, ed. Erkki Huhtamo and Jussi Parikka (Berkeley: University of California Press, 2011), 244.

2. For what I have learned about Updike and word processing, see my "Operating Systems of the Mind: Bibliography After Word Processing (The Example of Updike)," *PBSA* 108.4 (2014): 380–412, and *Track Changes: A Literary History of Word Processing*, 85–91 and 223–226.

3. Bowers, *Bibliography and Textual Criticism* (Oxford: Clarendon Press, 1964), 65.

4. It is also fundamentally Newtonian: the postulate essentially restates Newton's fourth law of reasoning. I owe this insight to David C. Greetham's invaluable essay, "Textual Forensics," *PMLA* 111.1 (January 1996): 33–34.

5. McKenzie, "Printers of the Mind: Some Notes on Bibliographical Theories and Printing-House Practices," in *Making Meaning: "Printers of the Mind" and*

Other Essays, ed. Peter D. McDonald and Michael F. Suarez, S.J. (Amherst: University of Massachusetts Press, 2002), 18.

6. McKenzie goes on to say as much: "the conception of 'normality' as a corrective to the undisciplined proliferation of generalizations misrepresents the nature of the printing process" (18). For a complete overview of McKenzie's championing of deductive method (and his indebtedness to Karl Popper in that regard), see Michael F. Suarez, S.J. "Extended Evidence: D. F. McKenzie and the Forms of Bibliographical Evidence," in *Books and Bibliography: Essays in Commemoration of Don McKenzie*, ed. John Thompson (Wellington: Victoria University Press, 2002), 36–56.

7. For a journalistic account of the emulation, see Devyani Saltzman, "Sniffing Through Salman Rushdie's Computer," *Atlantic* (April 21, 2010). The most compelling discussion of the emulation in a scholarly context is Porter Olsen, "Emulation as Mimicry: Reading the Salman Rushdie Digital Archive," *South Asian Review* 40.3 (2019): 174–189. Olsen explores the emulation from the standpoint of postcolonial theory and suggests that archives must be wary of reproducing colonialist dynamics in their curation practices—what critics such as Homi K. Bhaba have previously held up as forms of cultural "mimicry."

8. Martin Howse, *Diff in June* (Brescia: LINK Editions, 2013), np. Not incidentally, *Diff in June* is a print-on-demand book, a project that was feasible only under very specific technological conditions. Its title merges the operational program command that would have been used to generate the text—*diff*, short for difference, as in "what's the"—with a human measure of time.

9. All these things are possible of course, and indeed they happen routinely. But they are also generally instantaneously and transparently self-correcting. When glitches and errors do occur, they differ markedly and materially from the kinds of failures and frictions we encounter in the physical world (and to which bibliography itself is so marvelously attuned).

10. In truth, the question of accuracy in numerical calculation for manual and digital computing is quite vexed and has been throughout the history of computer systems design. The basis of most questions involves floating point arithmetic and rounding errors, wherein the placement of the decimal point (how it "floats") determines the values of integers. A watershed for the personal computer market was IBM's 8087 chip, which enabled its PCs to achieve the accuracy of much more expensive hardware designed for scientific use. (My thanks to Thomas Haigh for this detail.) See also (and not to be confused with the bibliographer), Donald MacKenzie, *Inventing Accuracy: A Historical Sociology of Nuclear Missile Guidance* (Cambridge: MIT Press, 1993).

11. Ellen Ullman, *The Bug* (New York: Doubleday, 2002), 345.

12. See Ginzburg, "Clues: Roots of an Evidential Paradigm," in *Clues, Myths, and Historical Method* (Baltimore: Johns Hopkins University Press, 1989), 94.

13. Ullman, 334, 340; emphasis added.

14. Ibid., 341–342.

15. Bowers, *Bibliography and Textual Criticism*, 64.

16. McKenzie, "Printers of the Mind," 63.

17. Kraus, "Conjectural Criticism: Computing Past and Future Texts," *Digital Humanities Quarterly* 3.4 (2009): 16.

18. I am thinking here too of the program Peter Stallybrass outlines in "Against Thinking," *PMLA* 122.5 (2007): 1580–1587.

19. Kraus, "Conjectural Criticism," 16.

20. Here I am relying heavily on the authority of Laura J. Snyder, "Sherlock Holmes: Scientific Detective," *Endeavor* 28.3 (September 2004): 104–108. Snyder writes: "Holmes also describes various 'rules of deduction' that he uses in reasoning backwards. These rules reflect common images of the work of Francis Bacon, the seventeenth-century philosopher of science whose writings became extremely popular in nineteenth-century Britain. Conan Doyle explicitly signals his appropriation of Bacon's method by having Holmes remark in *A Study in Scarlet* that the detective must reason as he does in order to 'interpret Nature,' a phrase famously used by Bacon in defining his own inductive method. (*Holmes' characterization of this method as 'the science of deduction' rather than 'the science of induction' is consistent with common usage of the term 'deduction' during the 19th century, when it was often used as a synonym for the more general term 'inference'*)" (108; emphasis added).

21. Ginzburg, "Clues," 92.

22. See my pages on the forensic imagination in *Mechanisms: New Media and the Forensic Imagination*, 249–259; see also Gallagher and Greenblatt, *Practicing New Historicism* (Chicago: University of Chicago Press, 2000), 20–48. My intent is not to align the forensic imagination with the New Historicism, but to acknowledge some affinities, including the forensically replete idea of foveation itself. For an early and important critique, see Alan Liu, "Local Transcendence: Cultural Criticism, Postmodernism, and the Romanticism of Detail," *Representations* 32 (Fall 1990): 75–113.

23. See Hartman, "Venus in Two Acts," and Lowe, *The Intimacies of Four Continents* (Durham: Duke University Press, 2015), 175.

24. See Kraus, "Conjectural Criticism."

25. The starting point for this critique is Leslie Howsman's early and important "In My View: Women and Book History," *SHARP News* 7.4 (1998): 1–2. More recently, see Kate Ozment, "Rationale for Feminist Bibliography," *Textual Cultures* 13.1 (2020): 149–178, and Sarah Werner, "Working Toward a Feminist Printing History," *Printing History* (forthcoming); Werner's text was initially delivered as the 2018 Lieberman Lecture, video of which is available online: https://www.youtube.com/watch?v=6liaqLStIdI.

26. Of course, not all users experience "access" the same way. Screen readers and other forms of adaptive technologies—beyond their essential practical utility—stand as reminders that even screens are contingent as opposed to inevitable modes of interface.

27. Douglas C. Hofstadter, *Fluid Concepts and Creative Analogies: Computer Models of the Fundamental Mechanisms of Thought* (New York: Basic Books, 1995), 488.

28. Ibid.

29. See my discussion of Magnetic Force Microscopy in *Mechanisms*, 58–69.

30. The speaker prior to me was Alexia Hudson-Ward. Audio of the complete plenary session is available at https://soundcloud.com/rarebookschool/bxd-plenary-3.

31. Please read my colleague Zita Nunes' interview with Richard Collins' mother, "Meanwhile He Is Loved . . . A Mother Grieves Her Murdered Son" (September 28, 2020): https://theblackcardcollective.org/meanwhile-he-is-loved-a-mother-grieves-her-murdered-son/.

32. See McKenzie, "The Book as an Expressive Form," in *The Book History Reader*, ed. David Finkelstein and Alistair McCleery (London: Routledge, 2002), 29.

33. A very partial and selective accounting of some doing the work would include: Brigitte Fielder and Senchyne, eds., *Against a Sharp White Background: Infrastructures of African American Print* (Madison: University of Wisconsin Press, 2019); Senchyne, "Under Pressure: Reading Material Textuality in the Recovery of Early African American Print Work," *Arizona Quarterly* 75.3 (Fall 2019): 109–132; Jordan E. Taylor, "Enquire of the Printer: Newspaper Advertising and the Moral Economy of the North American Slave Trade, 1704–1807," *Early American Studies* (Summer 2020): 287–323; Derrick R. Spires, *The Practice of Citizenship: Black Politics and Print Culture in the Early United States* (Philadelphia: University of Pennsylvania Press, 2020); Marcy J. Dinus, "'Look!! Look!!! at This!!!!': The Radical Typography of David Walker's 'Appeal,'" *PMLA* 126.1 (January 2011): 55–72; and Kinohi Nishikawa, *Street Players: Black Pulp Fiction and the Making of a Literary Underground* (Chicago: University of Chicago Press, 2018). This very partial listing is, it will be understood, narrowly focused on scholarship addressing chattel slavery and its aftermath in American print culture. It does not attempt to represent the larger cohort of scholars currently decolonizing book history and bibliography in a global context—a list McKenzie himself would join with his proto-post-colonial work on the Treaty of Waitangi in New Zealand; see "Oral Culture, Literacy, and Print in Early New Zealand: The Treaty of Waitangi," in *Bibliography and the Sociology of Texts* (Cambridge: Cambridge University Press, 1999), 77–130.

34. Fielder and Senchyne, "Introduction: Infrastructures of African American Print," *Against a Sharp White Background*, 5–6.

35. Quoted in Ira Berlin and the Students of HIST 429, "Knowing Our History: African American Slavery and the University of Maryland" (College Park: University of Maryland, 2009), 2. The Maryland Agricultural College (the institution that would become the University of Maryland) opened in 1859. The college's founder, Charles Benedict Calvert, was a slave-holder, as were most of the original trustees. Calvert was the patriarch of the family estate at nearby Riversdale; he was also a direct descendant of George Calvert, the Lord Baltimore, who on his death-

bed in 1632 was granted a Royal Charter by Charles I to the Native American land his descendants would colonize as Maryland. Records pertaining to the Maryland Agricultural College's construction were destroyed in a catastrophic fire on the campus in 1912, so full details regarding the labor of enslaved persons have been lost.

Acknowledgments |

Peter Stallybrass extended the invitation to give the Rosenbach Lectures over a dinner near the Folger Library in Washington, D.C. (he seemed to think I would need persuading). I am grateful to him and to the entire selection committee for one of the honors of my professional life. During my 2016 stay in Philadelphia, Peter as well as David McKnight, John Pollack, Will Noel, Dot Porter, Mitch Fraas, Priya Joshi, Zack Lesser, and Jim English all made me welcome. Jerry Singerman at Penn Press has been patient but persistent in the longish interval since: I thank him for his steadfast guidance and support. I am deeply grateful to the press's readers for their care and attention to my roughly hewn manuscript at what was no doubt a demanding time; they have contributed to this book in important ways. My sincere thanks also to the press's outstanding editorial, marketing, and production team.

One of the best advices I ever had comes by way of William Gibson's Cayce Pollard, though the original belongs to Theodore Sturgeon: "Always ask the next question." For answering *my* next (and next) questions, or for other kindnesses or assistances, or else for their example, inspiration, and friendship, I'd like to thank Sally A. Applin, Matthew Battles, Kathi Inman Berens, Charles Bigelow, David C. Brock (Computer History Museum), Brian Cassidy, Tita Chico, Andrew Clarke (Asia Pacific Offset), Lori Emerson, [Matthew] Farrell (Rubenstein Library), Andrew Ferguson, Andrew Ferguson (HyperCard Online), Neil Fraistat, Derek Freeman, Chris Funkhouser, Lisa Gitelman, Dene Grigar, Tom Haigh, Allison Hughes (Firestone Library), Grant Hutchinson, Paul Kepple (HeadCase Design), Deena Larsen, Susan Lynch (Melcher Media), Phil Madans (Hachette Book Group), Judy Malloy, Simone Murray, Laine Nooney, Brian O'Leary (Book Industry Study Group), Trevor Owens, Aaron Pratt (Ransom Center), Jessica Pressman, Leah Price, Rita Raley, Timothy Reiss, Russell Samolsky, Elaine

Savory, Jason Scott (Internet Archive), Jonathan Senchyne, Michael Suarez, Melissa Terras, Susan Tracz, Whitney Trettien, Sarah Werner, and Michael Winship. I am also grateful to the Andrew W. Mellon Foundation for its support of my *Books.Files* project, which contributed much to my writing in Chapter 3. A few of my paragraphs about William Dickey's HyperPoems previously appeared in a short essay written for the LitHub web site in November 2020.

Lecture invitations are seductive and easy to accept, a nice dinner or no; but books are the product not just of professional ceremony but also the ambient rhythms of day-to-day life, even or especially when these are disrupted in unforeseen ways. With this book, as always, I thank my parents Arlene and Mel, and the rest of my family. I especially want to acknowledge my supreme pride in my sister, Dr. Linda Kirschenbaum, and my brother-in-law, Dr. Charles Carpati, both critical care physicians in Manhattan who have been treating ICU patients since the onset of Covid-19. As always, my greatest debt is to my friend and life-companion, Kari Kraus, who (still) bears witness to the work, to the joys, and—as those ambient rhythms endure—to the harder things as well.

Two decades of academic life here at the University of Maryland have provided the foundation for my work in this book. My gratitude and my affection for my colleagues and students, present and past, is expressed in its dedication.

Index

Brathwaite, Doris Monica, 58–59, 63

Brathwaite, (Edward) Kamau: *Ancestors*, 64–65; colophons, 68; death, 41; Eagle, use of, 59, 60; life, 40, 58–59; Macintosh, use of, 40, 43, 60, 63, 64, 66–67, 71; *MiddlePassages*, 62–65; nation language, 59; Sycorax Video Style, 41, 60–67, 70–71, 127 n.85; typefaces, use of, 40–41, 43, 60–64, 71–73, 125 n.49, 126 n.57; writing and technology, thoughts on, 40–41, 59–60, 66–69

Caswell, Michelle, 25, 27, 29

Cerf, Vint, 22

China, role in the publishing trade, 75–76, 92, 129 n.5

Chun, Wendy Hui Kyong, 30–31, 33, 36, 37, 109, 120 n.39

cloud storage, x, 3, 9, 12, 30

Cohen, Matt, 72

Collins III, 2nd Lieutenant Richard W., 111, 137 n.31

colonialism in archives, 36, 72, 107, 135 n.7

colonialism in programming languages, 121 n.58

compatibility of digital files, 17, 33–35

computers and writing, 2–4, 6–7, 39, 40, 44–45, 50, 59, 66–68

convergence narrative, 81–82

Cook, Terry, 25, 29

Cooper, Dennis, *The Weaklings*, x, 115 n.3

Coupland, Douglas, *Microserfs*, 78–79

cyberspace, 25–26

Danielewski, Mark, 80, 130 n.17

Darnton, Robert, 76, 78

data centers, 3, 24, 30–32, 110, 118 n.17

data proliferation, 23–24, 100–102

deductive reasoning. *See* inductive vs. deductive reasoning

Derrida, Jacques, 24–26, 31

desktop publishing, 40, 56–58, 68. *See also* Adobe

Dickey, William H.: death, 41, 50; "The Education of Desire," 46, 48; *The Education of Desire*, 55; Hyper-Poems, 41, 46–56, 68, 123 n.27, 124 n.30; life, 39, 40, 44, 46; Macintosh, use of, 40, 45, 48–49, 51, 52; papers, 50, 52; posthumous publication of HyperPoems at Internet Archive, xii, 54, 124 n.30; writing and technology, thoughts on, 39, 40, 44–45, 48–50, 66–68

digital archival material, 12–13, 21–23, 29–33, 53, 117 n.4, 121 n.59. *See also* Dickey, William H.; Morrison, Toni

digital dark age, 22–23

digital materiality. *See* materiality of the digital

Doctorow, Cory, 5

Dorst, Doug. *See* Abrams, J. J., and Doug Dorst, *S.*

Doyle, Sir Arthur Conan, 106

Dropbox. *See* cloud storage

DuraBook, 86

dust, 15, 31–32, 38

Eagle computer, 59, 60

Eastgate Systems, 51, 55

Eisenstein, Elizabeth L., 57, 124 n.40

Eliot, T. S., *The Waste Land*, 1–2, 12–13

emulation software, 11, 12, 53, 54, 135 n.7

Microsoft Word, 2, 16, 17, 76, 89, 117 n.3, 118 n.4, 127 n.85

Morrison, Toni: *Beloved*, 15–20, 33–39, 117 n.4, 118 n.8, 122 n.61; papers, 15, 20, 21, 24, 32; revisions to closing lines, 18–20; writing and technology, thoughts on, 39. *See also* rememory

Moxon, Joseph, 78

Mr. Robot: Red Wheelbarrow, 86, 88, 92

Murray, Simone, 115 n.4, 131 n.20

Myst, 45

Neumann, John von, 7–8

New Directions Publishing, 62–65

New England Review / Bread Loaf Quarterly, 39

Novarese, Aldo, 62

QuarkXPress, 77, 79, 130 n.13

PageMaker. *See* Aldus PageMaker

Palladino, Robert, 43, 57, 124 n.36

Parham, Marisa, 35–36

PDF. *See* Adobe

Pentium bug, 103

planned obsolescence, 7, 26, 67, 101

Plant, Sadie, 11

Pool, Ithiel de Sola, 81–82

PostScript. *See* Adobe

postulate of normality, 99–100, 105, 134 n.4

preservation and materiality, 12–13, 27–28, 53, 120 n.49

Presidential Records Act, 22

Pressman, Jessica, 80, 83, 88, 131 n.19

publishing workflows, 4–5, 75–76, 78, 81, 92

Rainey, Lawrence, 1–2, 6, 13, 70, 101

Reed College, 43, 52, 57

rememory, 35–36, 52, 67, 72, 112, 121 n.59

Reynolds, Lloyd J., 43–44

right to be forgotten, 23

Rody, Caroline, 35, 118 n.5

Rushdie, Salman, 12, 101

Scott, Ridley, 41

secondary materiality, 90–91, 93

Shannon, Claude E., 8, 30, 70, 76, 81, 116 n.8

Ship of Theseus. See Abrams, J. J. and Doug Dorst, *S.*

Sterling, Bruce, 25–27, 29, 37

Sterne, Jonathan, 26, 82

Sterne, Laurence, *Tristram Shandy*, 133 n.35

ᔃCOP typeface, 62–65, 69, 72–73, 126 n.57, 126 n.62

storage media, 7, 9, 27–28, 33, 67. *See also* materiality of the digital

Stowe, Harriet Beecher, *Uncle Tom's Cabin*, 80–81

Stranger Things: Worlds Turned Upside Down, 87–88

supply chains, 75–76, 78, 81, 85, 86, 88, 93, 141 n.6

Sycorax Video Style. *See* Brathwaite, Kamau

TAR file format, 28, 119 n.34

Tom Clancy's The Division: New York Collapse, 86, 88, 92

transmedia storytelling, 80–81, 94–95

Trettien, Whitney, 115 n.6

TRON, 26

CPSIA information can be obtained
at www.ICGtesting.com
Printed in the USA
JSHW050222140921
18668JS00002BA/212